It's How Much You _KEEP_, That Counts! Not how much you Make.

THE _ULTIMATE_ TAX-REDUCTION SYSTEM
for Small & Home-Based Business

**THE _ULTIMATE_
TAX-REDUCTION SYSTEM™
"in a Nutshell"**

Congress has told the IRS to _Pay HUGE Refunds_ to taxpayers <u>who have a small or home-based business</u>!

* If, at **any time in the past 3 years**, you had a home-based business, you may qualify for **THOUSANDS of Dollars in TAX REFUNDS**, _Plus Interest_!

* If you have a home-business **now**, you probably can **slash your taxes** by **50%** _or more_ **this year**!

* **If** you are a traditional wage-earner and also have a home-business, you can probably **increase your take-home pay by hundreds of dollars** per month, starting immediately.

Ronald R. Mueller, MBA
and Scott C. Turner, CPA

ISBN 0-9707538-2-9

Printed in the United States of America

Cover Design
by
Michael Cartwright
mcgrafix@swbell.net

Table of Contents

It's How Much You KEEP, That Counts! <u>Not</u> how much you <u>Make</u>
Second Edition   © 2001

It's How Much You KEEP, That Counts! Not how much you Make
Second Edition © 2001

Appendices

It's How Much You KEEP, That Counts! <u>Not</u> how much you <u>Make</u>
Second Edition © 2001

Foreword
by
Robert G. Allen

For more than two decades I have been writing, lecturing, teaching and coaching thousands of people about the importance of establishing multiple streams of income. **I've been #1 on the New York Times bestseller list with two books:** Nothing Down and *Creating Wealth*, and my newest bestsellers are *Multiple Streams of Income* and *Multiple Streams of Internet Income*.

The media has referred to me as "the millionaire-maker" because of the great number of people who have taken my message to heart and acted on the advice I gave them.

Ron Mueller, the primary author of this step-by-step guide, is also one of my protégés and has been a close personal friend of mine for several years. The title of this book delivers a truly important message:

- No matter how many streams of income you put into place,
- No matter how large those streams grow to become,
- No matter how successful each stream turns out…

Ultimately, as it says on the cover,

It's How Much You *KEEP*, That Counts!
Not how much you Make!

This tax-reduction system is thoroughly-researched, carefully documented, fun to read and easy to use. In a word, **it is invaluable.**

With this book, anyone can understand and use all of the tax laws Congress has passed in order to encourage the average American worker to establish and run home-based businesses.

I'm not aware of any other book like this available anywhere.

Nothing this thorough, this uncomplicated, this useful.

"It's How Much You KEEP!" is a valuable addition to my own personal resource library. Congratulations to you for making it a part of yours too. But don't put this on your bookshelf. Use it! My own businesses are all based in my own home, for the very reasons Ron Mueller and Scott Turner describe in this terrific guide.

Do you want to know a secret? **A simple home-business offers more tax breaks than the super-wealthy can get with their expensive tax lawyers.** That's no lie!

You know, I've always thought that reading about tax-law was about as exciting as watching paint dry. But in this book, Ron and Scott actually make tax-law fun to read about! No kidding, you will actually enjoy reading this book! This is a "light read" with a "powerful impact."

Everyone with a home-based business needs this book! Anyone <u>without</u> a home-based business needs it <u>even more</u>!

Financial Freedom is an attainable goal. I think the most powerful way to accomplish it is to:

(a) Establish multiple streams of income
(b) Focus on streams that produce residual income
(c) Use the tax laws wisely in order to ensure that you are paying only the minimum required by law.

My books will help you with (a) and (b), but "It's How Much You KEEP, That Counts! Not how much you Make." is the book you need for (c).

Prosperously yours,

Robert G. Allen

Dedications & Acknowledgments

As Author, I would like to dedicate this book first of all to **GOD**, without Whom nothing is possible. A special debt of thanks goes to my good friend and personal mentor **ROBERT G. ALLEN**. His most recent bestseller, *Multiple Streams of Income*, and its phenomenal success, actually stimulated me to write this book. Everyone who reads Bob Allen's books and then follows his advice, will have one or more home-businesses, and thus be able to reap massive benefits from this new tax-reduction guide.

I also dedicate this book to my close friends **KEN KERR**, the creative genius behind Disney's EPCOT Center and now widely acknowledged licensing, direct marketing and advertising guru; and **MITCH AXELROD**, "trainer of trainers" in personal effectiveness, marketing genius, true humanitarian and my valued friend.

Finally, I acknowledge my parents **Clare and Betty Mueller** who instilled in me the core values of integrity, honesty and a sense of purpose – values that I hope are evident throughout this book; my son and daughter-in-law **Jeff and Jennifer Mueller** who shared in my excitement about publishing this book; my daughter **Christina Mueller** for her research assistance; my sister and brother-in-law **Lanette and Charlie Keever** and their son and daughter-in-law **Jason and Angie Mueller** who personally proved that following the advice in this book really does produce thousands of dollars in new tax savings; and my brother and my sister-in-law **Bob and Brenda Mueller** for their insightful questions and personal support.

Ron Mueller

AS CO-AUTHOR, I would like to dedicate this book to my remarkable children, **Garrett, Ben** and **Beth**; to my patient, loving mother **Fern Turner**, and to my compassionate, exemplar father **Duane Turner** – who all add incredibly to my life experience.

Scott C. Turner

New useful tax information is continually being posted on the Internet at www.HomeBusinessTaxSavings.com, so be sure to check it out frequently.

About This Book

By profession, the original author of this tax-reduction system is not a tax expert, a tax lawyer or a CPA (although I recruited THE best, in my opinion, as the book's co-author).

What I am is an investigative journalist. A journalist who asks good questions, who probes until I get answers that make sense, who follows up on every lead, who checks out every inconsistency, and who doesn't report anything until I thoroughly understand everything I can about the topic I'm writing about.

In 1999 I committed to a personal 'mission' to discover all the legal tax deductions available to part-time or full-time businesses run out of a taxpayer's home. **One of the first things I discovered, absolutely shocked me!**

It's a fact – expertise in home-based business tax law is not even tested in the CPA exam! Even CPA Continuing Education materials in most states have NEVER contained sections or offered courses regarding home-based business tax law.

Millions of Americans turn to CPAs for tax advice each year, assuming they know what deductions are legal and which ones are not. But just finding a person with the initials 'CPA' after his or her name, is no guarantee that he or she knows ANYTHING about home-based business tax law. They will <u>only</u> know it if they are <u>self-taught</u>.

As you will see in Chapter I, the key to maximizing your personal tax deductions (i.e., minimizing your legal tax requirements) is in operating a business based in your home.

Now I ask you, if most CPAs know <u>little</u> or <u>nothing</u> about home-business tax law, how many of them do you think are **<u>EXPERTS</u> in the many details of home-business tax law!?** As an investigative journalist, **I scoured the country and found only a couple dozen!**

It's How Much You KEEP, That Counts! <u>Not</u> *how much you* <u>*Make*</u>, is the result of extensive research, interviews, and synthesis of hundreds of written, spoken, published, authorized and/or approved tax-law interpretations and explanations by America's leading home-business tax-law experts.

The people whose works and words I studied and absorbed for a year and a half included home-business tax authorities such as retired career IRS Senior Executives, former IRS Investigators, a former top lawyer in the IRS' Office of the Chief Counsel, co-author of one of the most widely used tax-preparation software programs, **and a licensed CPA for more than 20 years who personally has served thousands of clients who own and operate their own home-based businesses.**

That CPA with over 20 years experience, and master of home-business tax law, ultimately became the **co-author of this Second Edition - Scott C. Turner, CPA.**

After running my own home-business for a full year, and using my hard-won knowledge to slash my own taxes by thousands of dollars, I knew I was ready to offer these insights to the millions of Americans who operate a home-based business and who have been needlessly over-paying their taxes year after year.

To them I say,
> **Pay Uncle Sam every penny required by law.**
> **But the law does not require you to over-pay!**

If you read about some deductions in this book that intrigue you, and then go ask your own tax preparer about them, he or she just may say, "No, that's not legal." Why? **Because they don't know!**

Why don't they know? To refresh your memory, skip back a couple pages. They've never studied it or learned about it.

12

You shouldn't have to fight with your tax preparer about the legality of these deductions, so here's what you will find throughout this book…

> **For every major deduction we describe in this guide, you will find, right here in black-and-white, the exact Congressional Law, Article in the U.S. Tax Code or United States Tax Court Ruling which specifically authorizes it.**

So, when your tax preparer says one of these deductions is not legal, point them to the source <u>cited in this book</u>. When he or she reads the sources we cite for you, he or she can arrive at only one conclusion – **the deductions are 100% legal, ethical, safe and proper.**

It's not their "fault" they didn't know about them. They never had an incentive to learn home-business tax law – that is until now.

But now you, their client, will say to them:

> *"I want to take advantage of far more deductions than you've ever told me about before, and I can prove that each one is legal and ethical."*

If you don't have a home-based business, you need one in order to qualify for these tax breaks. Send us an email at Info@HomeBusinessTaxSavings.com, and we will recommend some that allow you to take the fullest advantage of these tax laws.

Here's Proof that
These Strategies Work

My name is Blake Warrington. I'm a firefighter in Northern California, but also I have been an entrepreneur and home-based business owner for over eighteen years now. I am proof positive that the strategies detailed in this book do, in fact, work. I continually utilize these legal business deductions in my own home-based business on a daily basis – and so should you. In fact, if you are not, you are flushing your hard-earned money down the drain, just as I used to do.

For years I over-paid my taxes because I did not know the strategies that are so clearly described in this tax-reduction system. There was no guide like this available anywhere, and nobody ever shared this information with me – not even my CPA.

Let me show you how powerful the information contained in this book can truly be by sharing some of my personal 1999 Federal Tax Return information with you.

Once I projected how my home-based business would do financially that year, I was able to immediately change my W-4 form with my employer and claim seven allowances (you will understand more of what this means later in this book).

Claiming these additional withholding allowances **immediately increased my take-home pay from my regular job by a couple hundred dollars per month!**

By the end of the tax year for 1999 I had paid total Federal Income Taxes of just $7,276, which was only 10.88% of my total wages, salaries, tips (line 7 of my Form 1040).

15

But it turned out that I was too conservative on my W-4, because **I received a refund check in the amount of $5,141** of the $7,276 I had paid -- meaning that, in the end, I paid only $2,135 in Federal Income Taxes. In other words, *__my legal tax obligation was a mere 3.19% of my total wages__*.

I have had three IRS audits during my business career. In my first audit I ended up paying a couple hundred dollars for honest errors I had made. But because of the strategies contained in this book, and the fact that I now keep better records **(see Chapter X of this book),** my last two audits were stamped "Accepted as Filed."

In other words, all my deductions were found to be true and correct and I did not have to pay a penny in additional taxes!

Remember, my main intent (as well as yours), and the reason our government approved these legal tax breaks, is because they hope that we will all build large profitable businesses which will eventually pay more and more taxes. It's a win-win situation for everybody.

It is so important that every working American start a home-based business with the intent to make a profit, and begin to **implement these legal tax strategies immediately.** Don't put it off any longer. Read this book, get your business started, and *increase your take-home pay right away while you work towards creating that successful business!*

Blake Warrington

About the Authors

Ronald R. Mueller is a graduate of the United States Naval Academy in Annapolis, MD, where he earned a B.S. degree with majors in Management and Psychology. He later earned a Masters Degree in Mass Communication from the University of Oklahoma (including coursework at the University of Georgia), and then completed work for his Masters in Business Administration (MBA) at The George Washington University in Washington, DC.

Following Naval Academy graduation, Ron elected to serve his country on active duty as a Naval Officer for eight years, including a tour in-country during the Vietnam Conflict. He later retired from the Naval Reserve with 26 years service, at the rank of Captain (O-6).

Ron Mueller has been a newspaper reporter, an editorial writer, a television news producer, a magazine columnist, and a radio station DJ and newscaster.

He also has produced a record album, made TV commercials, recorded radio "spots," and written public education brochures, special inserts for newspapers, speeches for corporate executives, and strategies for major communications announcements.

His career has also included holding senior executive positions in businesses ranging from as small as a dozen employees to companies as large as a French-based multi-national consortium and a major Fortune-50 U.S. aerospace and defense contractor.

In 1999, Ron Mueller said "no more" to his grueling 4-hour-per-day, 100-mile roundtrip commute, and established his own home-based business – researching and writing this book.

Scott C. Turner graduated with a Bachelor's Degree in Business (with an emphasis in Accounting) from California State University at Hayward, one of the nation's top accounting schools.

Following graduation he was recruited by all 8 of the "Big-8" accounting firms. He accepted an offer from Main LaFrentz, a unit of KPMG, the largest accounting firm in the world, where he immediately specialized in Small and Home-Based Business accounting and taxation – a specialty in which he has remained focused to this day, more than two decades later.

He later left KPMG, was Certified as a Public Accountant (CPA), and joined a San Francisco Bay Area accounting firm, still specializing in small and home-based business taxes.

Scott Turner is the former Director of Tax Consultation Services for the nation's second largest employee benefits provider, now serving more than 8 million employees nationwide.

He also was a key member of the National Tax Team and was a Director of the Affiliate Organization for a business which provided tax consultation and audit representation for tens of thousands of American home-business owners.

Scott Turner manages a tax and accounting firm representing thousands of clients all over the United States, but stays focused on his specialty -- **Small and Home-Based Business Tax Law.**

Overview

Everybody thinks they are paying too much in taxes, yet it is a rare person who <u>does</u> anything about it.

Congratulations! By purchasing this book, you put yourself into the 1% of the population willing to at least **consider** taking some actions to legally reduce your taxes.

Let me ask you a question: If someone offered to show you a legal way to reduce your **mortgage** or **rent** payments by 50% or reduce your car payment by 50%, would you be interested? Of course!

Why, then, does 99% of the population take no action when offered information on how to reduce their **taxes** by 50%?

The two main reasons are:
(1) Fear of the IRS, and
(2) Fear of the time it will take to keep detailed records.

There's good news for you on both counts!

No Need to Fear the IRS

If you're not shoplifting, for example, do you care about those detectors at the exit door of the drug store? Why would you? If you're driving and have not been drinking, do you fear being stopped by police at a Breathalyzer checkpoint? No, because you have nothing to fear if you haven't been drinking.

When you obey the law, there is no reason to fear law enforcement.

Well, if you follow tax strategies passed into law by Congress and authorized in the IRS Code, would you have reason to fear an IRS audit? Of course not.

Look, if the speed limit is 55 mph, would you "play it safe" by driving 40 mph? **No!** Well then, why would you "play it safe" and decline to accept legal tax deductions passed by Congress for your benefit?

Your chance of being audited is less than one-half of one-percent, but even if you *are* audited, you have nothing to fear because "you're not shoplifting" and you're not "drinking while driving."

You are well within the law because every tax deduction in this book is 100% legal.

For people who carefully follow this tax-reduction system and get tax advice from experts on home-business tax law, an audit would simply be an inconvenience – not something to be feared.

Record Keeping is a "Piece of Cake"

This book will show you how to spend only minutes a day keeping records that could qualify you for up to $5,000 <u>or</u> <u>more</u> in tax deductions every year, **and** that also satisfy all the IRS requirements for documentation.

That's thousands of dollars in **your** pocket that you **have** been putting into **Uncle Sam's pocket** by over-paying your taxes.

There is <u>another</u> way to put an extra $5,000 in your pocket…

You could take-on another part-time job. But you would have to make $12.50/hour and work 10 hours a week, 50 weeks a year, to put $5,000 after-tax cash into your pocket.

Or, you could spend a few minutes a day doing record keeping at home, whenever it is convenient for you, instead of working two hours every weeknight for a full year at a part time job you'd most likely hate.

Financially, the result is the same either way. Which would you rather do?

As you read this book, you're going to discover that it is amazingly easy to qualify for thousands and thousands of dollars in legal tax deductions that you had no idea about before.

This Book is NOT about 'loopholes, 'tax-dodges' or 'gray-area deductions.'

Every deduction discussed in this book is specifically authorized by an Act of Congress, an Article in the Tax Code, or a Tax Court Ruling. Think about it, the laws themselves allow so many legal deductions for home-business operators, who needs to take-on the risky ones? Not you and not me!

We just discussed why you should have no fear of the IRS. First, the chance of an audit averages only one-half of one-percent – that's 1 out of every 200 people. Second, even if you end up being the '1' out of the 200, it'll be an easy audit, since you now have the specific reference authorizing every single deduction you claim, right here in this book.

Chances are, you'll be more knowledgeable than the IRS Auditor, which most likely will cause him or her to very quickly fold their books, and rubber-stamp your Tax Return:

Accepted as Filed

Why? Because the purpose of an audit is simply to see if a taxpayer qualified for all the deductions he or she claimed. By following the advice in this book, you will be able to very quickly establish that with the Auditor.

The Auditor's job is to identify people who are trying to cheat on their taxes, and then to collect the money they should have paid the government in the first place (plus interest and penalties).

Why would an Auditor want to waste his or her time going over the Tax Return of a taxpayer who can very quickly establish that he/she understands the tax laws, has followed them carefully, and has kept the required documentation?

They will "Thank you for your time," and go drop their fishhook in a different pond.

If you know of organizations whose members would benefit from this book, the publisher will offer you a generous "referral fee." Just send us an email at Info@HomeBusinessTaxSavings.com.

Chapter I

The United States Has TWO Tax Systems

(and You're Probably in the WRONG ONE!)

The United States has one tax system for **employees**, which includes most working Americans, and a very different, much better tax system for **businesses**.

Employees get to write-off **almost nothing**, but **businesses** get to write-off **almost everything**.

> **In this Guide, you will learn how you, as an *individual*, can legally and easily qualify for nearly all of the same tax breaks *businesses* get year after year!**

First, a little background on America's tax system. Or, we should say, tax system**S**, since we have just said there are **two** tax systems in America.

The first type of Taxpayer is the
Employee

Employees, or W-2 wage earners, work for someone else. Most taxpayers fall into this category. They have very few tax deductions available to them, usually just

- Mortgage interest,
- Standard deductions for dependents,
- Gifts to church or charity, and
- Contributions to a retirement plan.

Essentially, for employees, it's a three-step process:

Step 1: Work hard to earn a decent wage.
Step 2: Immediately lose a huge chunk of those wages to taxes.
Step 3: Then you get to take home whatever is left after taxes are paid.

The Second Type of Taxpayer is the
Business Owner

Business Owners, on the other hand, get to write-off just about everything from rent to phone bills to furniture and janitors, and even their coffee and donuts!

Business Owners have a **very different** three-step process:

Step 1: Earn money.
Step 2: Spend whatever they want or need to.
Step 3: Then pay taxes only on whatever is left over.

The long list of deductions available to **Business Owners,** include:

- Mortgage interest or Rent

- **Gas, electric, water and sewer**

- Cleaning crews to dust, vacuum and empty the trash

- **Computers, copiers, fax machines and telephones**

- Paper, pens, ink cartridges and even postage

- **Desks, sofas, coffee tables and other furniture**

- Painting, wallpaper, carpeting and other repairs/remodeling

- **Phones bills, cell-phones, pagers and Palm Pilots**

- Newspapers, magazines, books and on-line media

- **Plane fares, hotel costs, meals and rental cars**

- Lunches, dinners, ball games, theater tickets & health clubs

- **Security alarms, hidden cameras and guard dogs**

- Health, life, dental, vision, disability and unemployment insurance

- **Company cars (and even boats)**

- Gifts to charity, non-profits, libraries, etc.

- **Contributions to Employee Retirement Plans**

- Lawn mowing, landscaping, snow and leaf removal, driveway repair

- **Holiday cards, gifts and postage.**

- And just about any other expense that qualifies as "ordinary and necessary" to operate their business.

If You are an *Employee*, How Much are You *REALLY* Paying in Taxes?

The answer will astound you!

Taxes represent the single largest bill the average American employee pays! Every single payday, the amount withheld from your paycheck for taxes <u>before you even see it</u> is probably more than your <u>food</u>, <u>clothing</u> and <u>transportation</u> **combined**!

When you add together Federal taxes, State taxes, sometimes County or City taxes, Social Security taxes, Medicare taxes and all the rest, if you're like the "average" wage earner in America, **you pay 37.6 percent of your hard- earned wages in taxes, before you even see your paycheck.**

Now, most people believe in paying their "fair share" of taxes, but do you think that nearly 40% is your fair share?

The late Arthur Godfrey once said, "I'm proud to pay my taxes. But I'd be just as proud to pay half as much." Me too!

Do You Know WHY our Government uses "Payroll Deduction" as its Method of Collecting Income Taxes?

Here's an educated guess…

What if you received $1,000 in every paycheck, and then as soon as you got it you immediately had to write a check to the government for $376 for your taxes (37.6%), leaving you only $624 out of $1,000 to live on? What do you think would happen?

There would be a taxpayer revolt that would make the Boston Tea Party look like child's play, that's what would happen!

So what does our government do? They make your employer withhold all those taxes from your wages first, and then just give you the part that is left over.

That way, they're hoping you won't realize how much of a huge bite Uncle Sam is taking out of your pay!

Now, IMAGINE for a Moment...

How much less would you pay in taxes if you only had to pay Uncle Sam a percentage of **your "leftover money,"** like businesses do, instead of paying a percentage of the gross wages you earn, like you do now? You would pay a whole lot less in taxes, that's for sure!

What if the IRS would let you treat your <u>home</u> like an "office-building space" (which is tax-deductible), and what if they would let you treat your personal living expenses like "business expenses" (which are also tax-deductible)? Do you think that would make a difference in the taxes you pay?

Yes, a major difference!

Here's the Good News
You Have Been Waiting For!

It **is** possible for an **individual** to get most of the **same tax breaks** as business owners get!

But before we continue, I have to ask you an important question...

Would you mind if it turned out to be both 100% legal and really **EASY to cut your taxes in half?** Would it be okay if what I'm about to share with you is not at all complicated?

I'm serious. Some people really believe, "No pain, no gain." And many believe that if it has to do with taxes, "if it's easy and legal, 'my tax guy' would have told me about it." Don't believe either one. They're both wrong, as you soon will discover for yourself.

But first, let me share with you a story that I'm told is true.

Back when Coca Cola was a new company, their total business was selling syrup to "soda fountains," which then combined it with carbonated water to make a soft drink called a "Coke."

One day a visitor called on the Chairman of the Coca Cola Company in Atlanta, and said to him:

> *"If you decide to act on the idea I am about to share with you, will you give me one-half of one percent of the profits you make from it?"*

The Chairman agreed, of course, because if the idea was a good one, he'd gladly pay ½ of 1%, because Coca Cola would still get to keep 99½ %. And if the idea wasn't any good, it wouldn't cost him anything. So the visitor leaned over and whispered these two words:

"Bottle it."

Those two words very quickly made the visitor a multi-millionaire.

Was the idea complicated? **Of course not.**

Was the idea powerful? **<u>Absolutely</u>**!

Why did I want to tell you that little story? Because, just like "Bottle it," what I am about to share with you is not complicated, but is very, <u>very</u> powerful!

What's the easiest, and most powerful, way to slash your taxes in half or more?

Well, let's see…

A.   If a **Home** and **<u>Personal</u> Expenses** are **not** tax-deductible, but

B.   If a **Business** and **<u>Business</u> Expenses are** tax-deductible, the obvious conclusion is…

C.   **Your Home**
     + Owning a Business
     _____

          = *Tax-Deductible HOME BUSINESS!*

Your **home**, as the location of your business, becomes just as tax-deductible as a suite of offices in a high-rise office building.

And the expenses associated with that business, are just as deductible as the expenses associated with an "office-based" business.

[IRS Code, § 290 A]

If you're wondering when this amazing new set of tax laws were passed and why you haven't read about them, let me surprise you: **Nothing in this book is new**. Seriously! These Tax Laws, Tax Codes and Tax Court Rulings have been in place for years, in most cases.

But when you've finished this book, you will have a thorough understanding of two things that the vast majority of American taxpayers do not understand in the least:

- Exactly what the tax laws allow, and
- How to qualify to use them to reduce your own taxes to the legal minimum.

This information, as you will soon learn, is potentially **worth hundreds of thousands of dollars to you over your lifetime.**

Some people who already have a home-based business, find that they need to add an additional home-based business in order to qualify for all of the tax-deductions outlined in this manual. If you'd like some recommendations on home-based business that will help you maximize your deductions, just send an email to: Info@HomeBusinessTaxSavings.com.

Chapter II

A Home-Based Business Can Legally Qualify You for *Thousands* in Tax Breaks!

That's the equivalent to "Bottle it," as we discussed in Chapter I. It's **uncomplicated** like "Bottle it." And it is as **powerful** as "Bottle it!"

But many people who don't have a home-business usually don't want to start one. Why? They're too busy at their job trying to earn enough after-tax money to make ends meet. You have a job, right? You know what the word JOB stands for, don't you? My friend and best-selling author Robert G. Allen, who wrote the Foreword to this manual, says a J.O.B. stands for **Just Over Broke!**

First we chuckle at that, but then we realize it's TRUE! For many of us, the word should be spelled **JUB** for Just **Under Broke** since, most months the 'outgo' exceeds the 'income' and debt continues to climb.

That's why the Average American Household today holds 2.5 jobs! Isn't that sad?

But it doesn't have to be this way!

You are about to learn several things you didn't know before, and you are about to discover that several things you thought you knew about home businesses and the tax law, just are not correct. For example:

MYTH #1:

> *"My CPA told me that I have to show a profit in two out of every five years, or else I'll lose all my tax-deductions."*

TRUTH:

> That's what the IRS calls the "hobby loss rule." But you don't have "an income-producing hobby," you have a **business**. What's the difference? For one thing, to qualify as a bona fide business, you only have to prove your **intent** to produce a profit. You can claim losses year after year when you show that you have the **intent** to produce a profit.
>
> **[IRS Regulation 1.183-2(b)]**

NOTE: In just a few pages, we'll show you exactly how to prove your 'profit intent.' A simple Business Plan is one key to satisfying many of the IRS's requirements. See Appendix F for a draft of a simple Business Plan that meets all IRS criteria.

You've heard of Amazon.com, right? How many millions have they lost, and for how many years? They got to write-off all those losses for all those years on a row, **why**? Because they proved they had the **intent** to produce a profit, <u>and you can too</u>!

MYTH #2:

*"I can only write-off a room and the equipment and furniture in it if I use it **exclusively** for my business."*

TRUTH:

That's the IRS's "Exclusive Use Rule." As you'll soon learn, that restriction applies primarily to home-businesses providing only *Services*, as opposed to home-businesses which also market *Products*.   **[IRS Code, § 280 A(c)(2)]**

Also, "incidental personal use" does not negate the Exclusive Use Rule. (i.e., You could use your <u>business</u> computer occasionally to check sports scores or to send an e-mail to a friend without running afoul of the Exclusive Use Rule.)

MYTH #3:

"I've been told that the amount of my write-offs can't be any greater than the amount of money I make in my home-business, so if I'm not making much from my home-business, why bother with all of this?"

TRUTH:

Whoever told you that (maybe your own uninformed CPA!), only told you half the story. The truth is this: In <u>only one category</u> (called Indirect Expenses) the amount of write-offs can't be any greater than the total revenue from your home business (although losses in excess of revenue <u>can</u> be rolled-forward for use in a <u>subsequent</u> year).

However, many, many **other** expenses may be deducted well **in excess of the revenue** from the home-based business.

It is quite possible, for example, for a person running a home-business that produces only $1,500 in revenue, to be able to legally claim tax deductions worth up to $5,000 or even more. It all depends upon your specific circumstances, which we'll discuss later in this book.

"<u>Intent</u> to Produce a Profit." How Can You PROVE it to the IRS's Satisfaction?

Any company, including the one based in your home, can legally write-off business <u>losses</u> year after year, in many cases, when you show you have the INTENT to produce a profit.

The requirements are not difficult to meet, when you know what the IRS looks for, which we are about to reveal.

IRS Tax Auditors use EIGHT *SECRET "RELEVANT FACTORS"* to determine whether or not YOUR business has an "intent to produce a profit."   [Source: IRS Regulation 1.183(b)]

Well, They are NOT 'Secret' Any More, because HERE THEY ARE!

1. **Expertise of the Taxpayer or his/her Advisors.**

   You, personally, do not have to be an expert, even in your own business category, in order to satisfy this "relevant factor." If your company provides conference call 'training calls' and you participate in them regularly (at least a few of them each month), your long-distance phone bill will document your "effort to establish expertise." If your business is an MLM and you "three-way" calls into your upline, these calls document your use of "Advisors."

2. **Time and Effort the Taxpayer puts into 'Running the Business.'**

   Five long-distance business-related calls all made on the same day, is not nearly as good as five calls made on separate days. An "active" long-distance call log, receipts for postage, ordering of business promotional products and literature, etc. all provide evidence that the business is "active" and "ongoing."

3. **The Manner in which the Taxpayer Carries on the Business Activity.**

   If all of your "business activity" is conducted over lunch with friends or colleagues, or at sporting events, or at other places of entertainment, the IRS will likely be suspicious regarding your satisfaction of this "relevant factor." So hold meetings, make presentations, mail offer-letters, and have customers and prospects. In other words, actively run your business.

4. **Success of the Taxpayer in Carrying on Other Similar <u>or Dissimilar</u> activities.**

First of all, this is 1 of 8 "relevant factors" the IRS looks at, so if you meet the other 7 criteria, but not this one, in all likelihood this one will be "overlooked." This "relevant factor" does <u>not</u> mean that, in order to deduct expenses associated with your current business, you must have been profitable conducting a business in the past. What this does mean is that you are able to show that you've been financially successful at <u>something</u> business-related in the past. This "relevant factor" will not likely be considered relevant if this is your first attempt to run a home-business.

5. **Expectation that Assets Used in the Business Activity may Appreciate in Value.**

What this means is that if your business becomes very profitable over time, the assets of the company will likely be worth more (appreciate in value). But don't get hung up on this "relevant factor," because it is the most <u>subjective</u> of the factors, and thus should carry the least weight.

6. **Taxpayer's History of Income or Loss with respect to the Activity.**

If you run the same business (the "Activity") year after year, and it loses money year after year, you're going to have a hard time satisfying this "relevant factor." So, if your business has lost money for three or four years or so **in a row**, and if the amount of the loss is not decreasing, then **change businesses**.

If your "losing" business is an MLM, try a different MLM or an <u>additional</u> MLM, for example. Then the counter starts over regarding "number of losses in a row" because you'll be starting a **new** business.

40

7. Amount of 'Occasional Profits,' if any.

If you write-off $30,000 a year in business expenses, year after year, but once every few years you show a "profit on paper" of $200, the IRS will likely question whether the Activity is in-place with an "intent to produce a profit," **or** with "an intent to produce tax write-offs."

Use common sense. Congress gave us these "tax breaks" in hopes that some of us would start businesses that would become extremely profitable – and, thus, we'd become big tax-payers. So if your business does not show a reasonable profit at least some of the time, change businesses. (See answer to Factor 6, above.)

8. Elements of Personal Pleasure or Recreation.

Okay, pretend you are an IRS examiner. If a taxpayer deducts his golf club greens fees, theater tickets, dining expenses, vacations (i.e., "business travel") and hockey tickets as business expenses, but shows minimal ability to meet the other 7 "relevant factors," what would you think? The answer is obvious. You'd think he's claiming to have a home-business, but only in order to write-off his "personal pleasure" and "recreation" expenses.

When deciding whether or not to deduct an expense or cost, ask yourself, "If I were an IRS Auditor, how would I interpret this?" The word "Reasonable" provides a great deal of useful guidance.

Re-read the above 'Relevant Factors' more than once. Through them the IRS provides great insight regarding how you must set-up and conduct your home-business, so that you can qualify for the full range of tax advantages available to you.

Follow These Steps and
You Will Meet
the 8 'Relevant Factors'

STEP 1:   **Have a "Business Plan."**

This is, by far, the most important step in addressing all 8 of the IRS's "Relevant Factors." This is not as difficult as it may seem, because in the back of this book (Appendix F) we provide you with your own fill-in-the-blanks template for producing your own IRS-qualifying Business Plan.

STEP 2:   **Keep up with changes.**

Tax Laws, Tax Law Interpretations and Tax Court Rulings are in constant motion. That means home-business tax-law is continually being clarified, modified and changed. ***By owning this book, you qualify to receive FREE tax law updates FOR LIFE.*** See page 207 to learn how to enroll in this service <u>for free</u>.

STEP 3: **Document your activity.**

If the business you are in conducts Conference Calls for Training or Sponsoring, participate in those calls on a regular basis - at least once a week or so.

Why? Because the "Long Distance Call Detail" section of your phone bill will document, for the IRS, your "consistent efforts to learn and succeed in your business." This especially addresses IRS "Relevant Factor" #1.

STEP 4: **Order your company's products** on a regular basis for your own personal use, to use as samples and to use for "demo" purposes. Order promotional and marketing materials too. This will help you meet several of the IRS's "Relevant Factors."

SPECIAL NOTE: In Chapter XII we're going to show you how to put <u>extra cash</u> in your pocket <u>every month</u> from your "day job," just for having an active home-business. You will learn how to get Uncle Sam to essentially 'reimburse you' for spending $100 or so every month on your company's products AND to 'reimburse you' for up to <u>hundreds more</u> for marketing costs and other expenses associated with the running of your business.

STEP 5: **Have a customer-prospect list** –

and "work it," of course. Just having a list of names will satisfy half the IRS's requirements, and copies of your letters and e-mails to them, along with phone call notes, will satisfy the other half. This is easy - just click "save" on your computer every time you send a letter, memo, fax or email.

STEP 6: **Actively work your business.**

Be ready to show the IRS your business card, flyers you've posted or mailed, scripts you've used for telephone marketing and/or advertising you've run.

STEP 7: **Re-read this book** every couple months, at least at first, to make sure you understand all of the relevant aspects of home-business tax law.

STEP 8: **"Do not try this at home,"** as the saying goes. Even if you've been doing your own taxes for years, or if Uncle Harry always helps out, **use a <u>tax pro</u> to prepare your taxes**, and **<u>insist</u>** on one who **<u>specializes</u>** in **home-business tax-law**. (See page 203 if you need help finding one.)

Chapter III

How to Convert
Non-Deductible *Personal* Expenses
into
Tax-Deductible *Business* Expenses

The IRS now concedes that "a business is a business," no matter what its size, whether or not it makes a profit, or where it is located.

That means as the owner of a small, part-time business run out of your home you are to be treated no differently, for tax purposes, than the owner of a large business that is run out of a huge office building.

With a home-business, your <u>home</u> is your <u>office building</u>, and the costs to maintain it then become tax-deductible expenses.

What Exactly Are the
Personal Expenses You Can 'Convert?'

As you will see on the next page, it is a V E R Y long list!

Here's a <u>partial list</u> of just *some* of the tax-deductible expenses that businesses legally and routinely write-off, and just **some** of the HOME-business expenses that YOU can legally and routinely write-off, too.

[**IRS Code, § 280 A**]

Legal **Business** Deductions		Legal **HOME-Business** Deductions
✘	Mortgage Interest or Rent	✘
✘	Gas, Electric, Water and Sewer	✘
✘	Cleaning Crews to Dust, Vacuum and Empty Trash	✘
✘	Computers, Copiers, Fax Machines and Telephones	✘
✘	Paper, Pens, Ink Cartridges and even Postage	✘
✘	Desks, Sofas, Coffee Tables and other Furniture	✘
✘	Painting, Wallpaper, and other Repairs/Remodeling	✘
✘	Phones Bills, Cell-Phones, Pagers and *Palm Pilots*	✘
✘	Newspapers, Magazines, Books and On-line Media	✘
✘	Plane Fares, Hotels, Meals, Rental Cars while Traveling	✘
✘	Dinners, Ball Games, Theater Tickets & Health Clubs	✘
✘	Security Alarms, Hidden Cameras and Guard Dogs	✘
✘	Health, Life, Dental, Disability and other Insurance	✘
✘	Company Cars and even Boats	✘
✘	Gifts to Charity, Non-Profits, Libraries and Colleges	✘
✘	Contributions to Employee Retirement Plans	✘
✘	Grass Cutting, Landscaping, Snow Removal, etc.	✘
✘	Holiday Cards and Postage and Gifts	✘

It sure looks like the two columns of deductions are <u>identical</u>!

46

Of course they are identical! Remember that your <u>home</u> is your <u>place of business</u>, and "business expenses are business expenses," whether the business is "housed" in a high-rise office building or in a suburban home.

Let's look more closely at that list and see what it means in terms of tax savings...

Mortgage Interest or <u>Rent</u>

> Yes <u>Rent</u>! Finally, renters get a tax-break. Since business owners do not normally own the office building in which they are housed, why should you have to own the house in which your <u>home</u>-business is based? You shouldn't, and the Tax Court agrees. Renters may now claim a business rent deduction on their Schedule C according to the Business Use Percentage (BUP) of their home. The next section of this chapter shows you how to determine your BUP and how to maximize the number. **[IRS Publication 587]**

Please NOTE: 'Double Deductions' are available for some homeowners. Any taxpayer can claim Standard Deductions on their Form 1040 OR they may itemize their deductions on a Schedule A (Itemized Deductions). But, as a home-business owner, you'll now be moving many of your personal (Schedule A) deductions over to Schedule C (Profit or Loss from Business). This may reduce your Schedule A "write-offs" to almost nothing. If that is the case with you, consider <u>not</u> filing a Schedule A at all, and take advantage of the "Standard Deduction" option on your Form 1040.

Gas, Electric, Water and Sewer

Of course this not only includes the utilities themselves, but any equipment, repairs, service or maintenance. For example, a new heat pump or furnace, addition of a humidifier, salt for a water conditioner, plumbing repairs, well-pump replacement, fall furnace tune-ups, chimney cleaning, duct cleaning, etc. See Chapter IV for specifics on how much you can deduct.

[IRS Publication 587]

Cleaning Crews to Clean your Office Space

This means you can hire your kids (tax-deductible to you, tax-free to them) to perform business services for you as "employees," instead of paying them a non-tax-deductible "allowance," which you'd pay out of your after-tax wages. (You'll learn specifics about how to do this in Chapter VI.)

Computers, Copiers, Fax Machines and Phones

Contrary to popular opinion, these items do NOT have to be used *exclusively* for business purposes, in order for you to be able to benefit from tax deductions. See next chapter for specifics on *how much* you can deduct.

[IRS Code § 280 F(d)(4) and IRS Publication 956]

SPECIAL NOTE: If you want details and examples regarding depreciation and tax write-offs regarding business furniture and equipment, as well as laws about converting currently owned furniture and equipment from Personal Use to Business Use, consult with a tax professional who specializes in home-business tax law. (See page 203 if you need help.)

Paper, Pens, Ink Cartridges and Postage

Of course these items, and all kinds of office supplies, are deductible for any business, <u>including your own</u> home-based business.

Desks, Sofas, Coffee Tables and other Furniture

The "rule of thumb" is "if you use it in your business, it's probably deductible." Think about a traditional business run out of an office building. Don't you think they are tax-deducting the cost of the sofa and coffee table in the lobby, the small round meeting tables and chairs in private offices, and even the coffee maker and water cooler in the kitchen? Of course, and <u>so can you</u>. See Chapter V for specifics on how much <u>you</u> can deduct.

Painting, Wallpaper, Carpeting & Maintenance

Many people think that "upgrades" are deductible but "routine maintenance" is not. *They're wrong.* That is the "tax rule" regarding deductibility of expenses associated with selling a home, but it has <u>nothing</u> to do with <u>home-business deductions</u>. As long as the room is used at least part of the time for business purposes, then at least part of the expense is probably deductible. See next chapter for specifics on *how much* you can deduct. **[IRS Publication 587]**

Phone bills, Cell-phones, Pagers and Palm Pilots

They're all deductible if they're used in your business, but there is one exception, and we'll cover that in detail later in this tax-reduction guide. **[IRS Publication 587]**

Newspapers, Magazines, Books & On-line Media

Again, if you need it for your business, it's probably deductible. You probably don't need *Reader's Digest* for your business, but you probably do need *Upline* magazine, or *Entrepreneur*, or even the daily newspaper since you probably check the Classifieds for competitive intelligence and read the news pages for current news about your product category or about your customers.

Plane fares, Hotel costs, Meals, Rental cars

Expenses related to business travel are usually deductible, so if you can combine your vacation travel with your business travel - and pay attention to the IRS rules - even 'vacations' can be deductible. (All the details are in Chapter VIII of this book.)

[IRS Code § 162(a)(2)]

Lunches, Ball Games, Theater Tickets & Club Dues

This is a tricky category, so please proceed carefully. This is **the** category in which most people are confused, so if you happen to get audited, the IRS will look into this one. But thousands of dollars worth of deductions are available under the right circumstances, so this is definitely worth learning about. (See details coming up in Chapter IX of this book.)

Health, Life, Dental and other types of Insurance

Under the right circumstances (which you can often create) you can deduct not only the cost of the premiums, but also the annual deductibles, co-pays, etc. (Chapter VI of this book spells out details.)

Security Alarms and Hidden Cameras

A business owner needs to protect his or her place of business, and the IRS recognizes that this is a normal cost of doing business (i.e., a legal tax deduction). **By the way, when you think "alarm system," think broadly.** If you install floodlights with motion detectors on your home (which is your place of business), you're installing a security alarm system.

[IRS Publication 587]

Company Cars and Even Boats

A car (or boat) does not have to be used exclusively for business purposes in order to be deductible. Chapter VII will blow your mind, because that chapter alone, will probably save you over 100 times what you paid for this tax-reduction system!

Gifts to Charity, Non-Profits, Libraries and Colleges

This category, frankly, is no big deal because individuals can claim these same deductions. Gifts from you as an individual can be claimed on Schedule A, but promotional gifts from your business can be claimed on Schedule C.

Contributions to Employee Retirement Plans

The rules are the same, whether you are an employee or a home-business owner.

Grass Cutting, Landscaping & Snow/ Leaf Removal

If you owned an office building, these costs would be deductible, right? The amount you can deduct for your home-business depends upon your "Business Use Percentage," which we'll discuss in the next chapter. **[IRS Publication 587]**

Holiday Cards, Postage and Gifts

They're deductible, as long as they promote your business. That could be done within the context of a Christmas Letter which many people insert in their cards, or you could simply have the card be signed, "Frank and Bonnie Smith and Smith Enterprises."

The vast majority of your *non-deductible* "personal" expenses suddenly can be converted into tax-deductible business expenses **when you PROPERLY set up your home-business,** which we'll cover **next**.

> **NOTE:** Tax Laws and Tax Court Interpretations are constantly changing. Buy owning this book, you qualify for a FREE subscription to "Tax Tips You Can Bank On." See page 203 to learn how to subscribe to this *FREE* service.

Chapter IV

MAXIMIZING
Business Deductions by Using
Your Home as Your Place of Business

Remember all those non-deductible personal expenses we just discussed converting into tax-deductible business expenses? Well, we cannot write-off 100% of those expenses, because, after all, we do live there too.

However, we can get as close to 100% as possible!

What dollar-amount or percentage of those expenses can you deduct? There are three categories of expenses, and different (but easy) methods for calculating each. The only three terms you'll need to understand are:

1. **Business Assets**
2. **Direct Expenses**
3. **Indirect Expenses**

BUSINESS ASSETS:

As you would expect, Business Assets include **business equipment** such as computers, fax machines, etc.; and **business furniture** such as desks, desk chairs, filing cabinets, etc. These assets are deductible at 100%, providing they are used exclusively (or *almost* exclusively) for business purposes.

But the list doesn't stop there. If customers, clients and/or prospects visit your place of business (your home), it would be customary to furnish a lobby (your living room) and perhaps a meeting room (maybe your den), and to have equipment available (such as a television set and a video or DVD player) for making business presentations.

The furniture and equipment in these rooms also are tax deductible (although not at a full 100%) because they too, are partially Business Assets. How much can you deduct?

Let's say (based on your best estimate or upon an "actual-use-log"), your sofa is used 7 out of every 10 times for business purposes, and 3 out of every 10 times for personal, family use. You would likely be allowed to deduct 70% of the cost of the sofa as **Business Asset.**

DIRECT EXPENSES:

Direct Expenses are expenses directly related to the conduct of your business. This category would include office supplies; telephone service; relevant newspaper and other subscriptions; cellular phones, beepers and pagers; security alarm monitoring fees; employee benefits; repairs and upkeep of rooms used exclusively for business purposes, and professional dues. Direct expenses generally are 100% deductible.

INDIRECT EXPENSES:

Rent, utilities, lawn care and general maintenance (such as replacing a roof or repainting the exterior of a house), are examples of *Indirect Expenses.* The amount of Indirect Expenses you can deduct depends upon the "Business Use Percentage" (BUP) of your home.

First of all, the '**P**' in BUP applies to a **Percentage of what?** It is the *finished* square footage of your home (i.e., it does not include such areas as your garage, barn, land, or unfinished basement or attic).

Lets look at an example…

Lets say your home has a Living Room, a Kitchen, a Dining Room, 3 Bedrooms, a Den and 2 Bathrooms. Now, lets say the Living Room, Den, Dining Room and one bedroom-office are all used in your business -- not strictly used exclusively for business, but used "regularly and primarily."

Let's say that, in square footage, those rooms make up 65% of the "finished" area of your home. Of course, you must have a restroom if your customers and prospects visit your business, so one of the bathrooms could also qualify. If so, now we're up to about 70%.

Your **Business Use Percentage (BUP)** then would be 70%. That means that ALL Indirect Expenses can become 70% tax-deductible.

Imagine that! Legally deducting 70% of your home heating and cooling bill, 70% of your rent (yes, RENT, not just mortgage interest!), 70% of your maintenance and upkeep costs, even 70% of your lawn care and snow removal expenses!   **[IRS Publication 587]**

How do you make your living room, for example, qualify for inclusion in the BUP? If you take samples of products that you sell, and display them on your coffee table, the IRS says you can deduct the square footage the coffee table occupies, plus "a reasonable amount of walking space" around it. (Of course, the coffee table *itself* may be a tax-deductible *Business Asset*, as we have just discussed.)

That's not much square footage, right? **But** what if we **also** display products on the <u>end table</u>, on top of the <u>piano</u>, on a <u>bookshelf</u>, on top of the <u>TV</u> and on a <u>windowsill</u>?

Suddenly you pretty much have the entire living room as a tax-deductible "showroom," don't you?

Let's work with that example…

Draw a rough pencil-sketch of your own Living Room here.

Now, take a colored marker or highlighter, and place a dot at every location where you **<u>could</u> display product samples.**

See how easy it is to turn the vast majority of your Living Room into a "Product Showroom?"

58

We at New Images first give Honor to God

We also thank our wonderful sponsors

Michigan Legislative Black Caucus
SBC Ameritech
IBM Corporation
Campus Ford
M&M Distributors
State Representative Virg Benero
State Representative Paul DeWeese
Lingg Brewer
MSU Extension
Davenport University
Capitol Cadillac
The East Lansing Center for the Family
Wilson & Delois Caldwell
Veronica Johnson
Cynthia T. Pugh
Dr. Michael & Bonita Murphy

Deborah Robertson – Gold Pages of Michigan
Music provided by Minister Ray Potter
Mr. Turkeyman Catering – Craig Harris, Greg Gibson
The entire staff of Bethlehem Church
The staff of New Images Production

ays his

e or she

ant this

to see

examples

onverted

e-off

ooms

and

80 A]

Iow often
do you use it for dining? If you're like most of us, you use it two,
maybe three, times a year, right?

59

If so, then don't think of it as a "dining room." Think of it simply as another room that you <u>need to use regularly in your business</u>.

Let's say you "regularly and exclusively" use your dining room to…

- Assemble mailings to your customers/prospects,
- Process your invoices and payments, and to fill out deposit slips, and
- Store and display the products you market.

The fact that you "clean up" that room twice a year to host a family Thanksgiving dinner or anniversary party does <u>not</u> negate the "Exclusive Use Rule."

The key words here are:

- **Ordinary**
- **Necessary** *and*
- **Reasonable**.

If you **Ordinarily** use the room on an "exclusive basis" for your business, if it is **Necessary** to use that room in the conduct of your business (in your opinion), and if it is **Reasonable** to conclude that the room is *primarily* used for business, that room could meet the BUP requirements.

> **Please Note:** The key word here is "**Reasonable**." Consider an office conference room that is occasionally used to throw a Baby Shower for an employee; that action does not disallow the conference room as a legitimate business deduction, does it? Of course not.

Are you catching the drift? Let the business e x p a n d to encompass as much of your home as is Necessary and Reasonable. Can you see why a mansion would probably have a much lower BUP than a small house?

How about the <u>non</u>-finished square footage of your real estate property? Let's say someone wanted to be able to legally tax-deduct some of the cost of repairing and repainting her barn. Now, a barn is not normally considered a part of the "finished area" of a home, so it would not be included in the BUP calculations. What would you have done?

What she could do is to simply begin storing her home-business product samples, inventory and supplies in the loft of her barn. What's another word she could now use for her "barn?" How about "warehouse," perhaps? Maintenance and upkeep of a business warehouse or storage area IS tax-deductible! Not the whole 100%, of course, but a "reasonable percentage."　　　　**[IRS Code § 280 A(c)(2)]**

Don't have a barn that needs repairs? How about the garage? The workshop? You get the idea.

Keep thinking like a business owner who rents an office building...

If an office building has a security alarm system, the costs of installation, monitoring and maintenance are fully deductible, right? Of course.

How about your home-business? Does your home have a home security alarm system? If so, the installation cost, maintenance and monitoring fees are tax-deductible.

You **don't** have a home security alarm system? Do you have a dog that barks whenever someone comes near the home/business? **Your dog could be your alarm system**.

Many auto-parts "junkyards" have "junkyard-dogs" for their "security systems." Both the owner of the junkyard <u>and you</u> could tax-deduct the costs of dog food, vet bills, vaccinations and yearly dog license, when the dog qualifies as your security alarm system.

[IRS Publication 587]

One more example… Would a business be allowed to legally deduct the cost of a pest control company coming in regularly to trap mice and other nasty critters?

Of course. Well…

Do you have a cat? Don't answer that too quickly! If they catch mice (or even if they scare them away) **what you <u>may</u> have is a "rodent control system."** If so, your cat food, vet bills, vaccinations and pet license, all may be tax deductible! Cats are cheaper than Terminex, and Terminex won't snuggle in your lap!

Note: Here's One Exception
to the BUP Formula

The IRS rules about deductibility of your **telephone bill** are a little bit different. [IRS Publication 587]

Your **<u>base</u>** phone charges are **not** tax deductible, <u>period</u>. "Base phone charge" refers to the amount you would pay if you had no long distance calls, no second line, no add-on services like call waiting, call forwarding, caller ID, 3-way calling, etc. The cost of minimal phone service = your "base phone bill."

Although your "base phone bill" is 0% deductible, your "add-on" services can be 100% deductible if you have them in order to facilitate the operation of your business, which of course is why you'd subscribe to these optional services, right?

Of course, every long-distance call must be annotated on your monthly phone bill as either a business call ("B") or a personal call ("P"). If you do business with all of your family and friends, then virtually all of your long-distance calls could be deductible. Just make sure the <u>primary purpose</u> of your call is to discuss <u>business</u>, and let the secondary purpose of your call be "personal chat." Do this, and all of your calls to family and friends can be legally deductible.

Suggestion: If you're in an MLM business, enroll family and friends in your "downline." You'll be able to easily prove the "business intent" of each long distance call.

Oh, by the way, who determines what the "primary purpose" of the call is? <u>You do</u>!

You Can Even Write-off Your RENT !

Yes, it is true! When you have a home-based business, you can legally deduct either the BUP of your mortgage interest **or your RENT**. It doesn't matter!

Does a 'traditional business' have to own its office space in order to deduct it? Of course not, so why should you? You don't.

Finally _renters_ can get the same tax deductions their home-buyer friends get! Is this a great country, or what?

So, since your home is your place of business, does it matter whether you own or rent your "office space?" Again, of course not!

You can deduct the "Business Use Percentage" of your mortgage interest **or** your rent payments, *either one*!

Deduct Newspapers, Domestic Help
and Gardeners too!

Yes, again, it's true! If reading newspapers and magazines is essential to running your home-business, which is highly probable, they are tax deductible expenses, just as they are for businesses based in office buildings.

Also, a traditional business can tax-deduct the costs of janitorial service, so likewise, the owner of a home-business can tax-deduct the BUP of house cleaning expenses.

Does a **traditional** business get to write-off the costs of landscaping, grass cutting, leaf and snow removal, driveway resurfacing, trash collection, etc., around the office building? Of course. Well, if the "business use percentage" of your home is 70%, for example, shouldn't **you** get to write-off 70% of **your** landscaping, grass cutting, leaf and snow removal, etc.?

The answer is a resounding **YES!**

Hold On, We Have <u>Barely Begun</u> Saving You Money on Your Taxes!

If you find **this** information amazing, just wait until you read the rest of this tax-reduction guide.

You are about to learn some tax reduction strategies your tax preparer probably hasn't even thought about – unless he or she is a seasoned expert in home-business tax-law. And rest assured that every single deduction is 100% legal. Remember, we're even citing the sources to prove it!

Pull out a pencil and grab a calculator and look over to the next page. Let's estimate how much of YOUR personal home expenses can be converted into YOUR tax-deductible business expenses.

▶
▶
▶
▶
▶
▶
▶

If you have difficulty finding a tax preparer who is experienced in home-business tax law, email us for help at Info@HomeBusinessTaxSavings.com.

Converting YOUR Personal Expenses into YOUR *Estimated* Business Deductions

Calculating Your "Business Use Percentage" (BUP)

1. Total *finished* square feet of your home = A: _____
2. Total square feet used in your business = B: _____
3. B ÷ A = BUP   BUP: _____ %

Estimating Your New Tax Deductions

Expense Category	ANNUAL Cost	Conversion Factor	Estimated Tax Deduction
Mortgage or Rent	$_____	x BUP%	$_____
Gas	$_____	x BUP%	$_____
Electric	$_____	x BUP%	$_____
Water/Sewer	$_____	x BUP%	$_____
Trash Collection	$_____	x BUP%	$_____
House Cleaning	$_____	x BUP%	$_____
Yard Work	$_____	x BUP%	$_____
Leaf/Snow Removal	$_____	x BUP%	$_____
Deck Treatment	$_____	x BUP%	$_____
Driveway Repairs	$_____	x BUP%	$_____
Security Alarm/Dog	$_____	x BUP%	$_____
Pest Control/Cat	$_____	x BUP%	$_____
Repairs/Maintenance	$_____	x BUP%	$_____
Business Supplies	$_____	x 100%	$_____
Postage and Courier	$_____	x 100%	$_____
Subscriptions	$_____	x 100%	$_____
Cards & Stamps	$_____	x 100%	$_____
Internet Access Fees	$_____	x 100%	$_____
Books/Magazines	$_____	x 100%	$_____
Cable TV Service*	$_____	x 100%	$_____
Phone Bills**	$_____	x 100%	$_____
Other	$_____	x ??%	$_____

▼   ▼

Current Expenses = $_____

Amount to be Converted into Business Deductions = $_____

* For channels related to running your business
** Excluding "base amount" for 1st phone line.

There Are Dollar-Amount-Limits
on SOME of these Deductions

Deductions for expenses falling into the **Indirect Expense** category (rent, utilities, repairs/remodeling, landscaping and a few others) are limited to the amount of revenue earned by your home-based businesses.   For example, if your home-business sold $4,300 worth of products during a tax-year, your total deductions <u>from these expenses</u> for that tax-year may not exceed $4,300.   Any additional deductions can be carried-forward for use in subsequent years.

HOWEVER, deductions for Direct Expenses and deductions for Business Assets *may* exceed the amount of revenue generated by your home business.

The next Chapter how that works…

Chapter V

Converting
"Personal Property" into "Business Assets"
and
Acquiring <u>New</u> Business Assets

As mentioned in the last chapter, an "office-building business" would be expected to have a sofa, coffee table, lamps, etc. in its lobby for the use of customers and prospects visiting the office, right?

If you have customers and prospects visiting your home-business, you have the same needs -- and the same tax deduction rights.

Let's use a sofa for our example. You could either "convert" a currently-owned sofa from "Personal Use" to "Business Use" or you could acquire a <u>new</u> sofa as a "Business Asset."

For "converting," the calculation goes like this...

First you determine the approximate value of your sofa at the time of conversion. Then you estimate the percentage of business-use versus personal use of the sofa. Next you multiply the value times the

71

percentage for business-use. The resulting number is then depreciated over a seven-year period.

An example will help to clarify…

> Let's say your sofa was purchased new for $1,000, and today it's worth about $700. And let's say out of every 10 times the sofa is used, 6 will be for business and 4 will be for personal use (thus, business use = 60%). Next you multiply $700 by 60%, and the result is $420. Now, since you are required to depreciate the "asset" over a 7-year period, you can claim 1/7th or more of $420 (which is $60+) on each of your next seven tax returns as Asset Depreciation.

The tax law is **much more liberal** when you **buy** a sofa for business use, rather than **converting one** from Personal use to Business use. By the way, it doesn't matter whether you purchase a new sofa or a used sofa. (Could this be a way to collect antique furniture while writing-off a large percentage of the cost?)

After your business is established, if you bought that same sofa for $1,000 (whether it was new or used), Uncle Sam actually gives you a choice of two methods you can use to get your tax benefits.

- You can choose to multiply the $1,000 by your 60% business-use (which = $600), and then depreciate that $600 amount over seven years. (Same as in the example above, except in this case you get an $85+/year deduction for Asset Depreciation instead of only $60+/year.)

72

--- or ---

- You can choose to deduct the entire 60% of the $1,000-purchase (which = $600) ALL in the year in which it was purchased.

If you need tax deductions this year, you might choose the second option, but if you do not need the deductions this year, the first option might be a wiser strategy. Be sure to consult with your tax professional **before** purchasing any asset that will be used in your business.

NOTE: **The depreciation period is only FIVE years for electronic equipment such as:**

- Computers and peripherals
- Phones and phone systems
- TVs, VCRs, DVD players, tape players and CD players
- Photo-copiers, fax machines, scanners and printers.

By the way, items of furniture or equipment which cost less than a few hundred dollars, may be considered as "supplies," and, thus, "written-off" as business supplies and not subject to the multi-year depreciation rules relating to business equipment and furniture.

For example, if you purchase a filing cabinet for $200, you do not have to depreciate it over a 7-year period, or if you purchase a new VCR for $300 you do not have to depreciate it over a 5-year period.

Don't forget…

In the example of the sofa discussed above, not only do you get a tax deduction for the sofa itself, but you can also include the square footage it occupies (plus "a reasonable amount of walking space around it") in the calculation of your BUP – the percentage number you use for writing-off utilities, rent, etc.

You might want to provide your tax advisor with a sketch of each room of your home, including dimensions of the rooms themselves and dimensions of the furnishings in them. He or she can then help you compute your BUP, and the depreciation for your "business assets."

74

Chapter VI

Employ Your Family Members, then Watch Your Tax Deductions SOAR!

HIRE your Kids
Instead of Paying them an Allowance!

Can a business write-off the costs of janitorial service? Of course!

[IRS Code § 162(a)]

Since you have a business based in your home, hire your kids to vacuum, dust and take out the trash.

[Tax Court Memo 1991-50 in Jordan v. Commissioner of the IRS]

The expense is tax-deductible to you, and the income is tax-free to them.

[IRS Regulation 1.162-7(a)]

The limit was $4,500 per child for year 2001 and is $4,700 for 2002. The amount is equal to the "Standard Deduction."

[Rev. Proc. 95-53 and IRS Code § 63(h)(2)]

The only limitation is that they must be at least 6 years of age.

[Tax Court Ruling in Eller v. IRS 77TC934; Acq. 1984-2 C.B. 1]

And, if they are family members under 18, they are exempt from payroll taxes **[IRS Code § 3121(b)(3)(A) and § 3306(c)(5)]** and the business is not required to withhold or to pay Social Security and Medicare taxes. **[Tax Court Ruling 48 TC 439, 450 (196) in the case of Denman v. IRS Commissioner]**

In order to audit-proof this aspect of your home-business deductions, use a formal Employment Contract to hire your family members. You'll find a sample fill-in-the-blanks Employment Contract in Appendix B in the back of this book.

In order to qualify, the wage-rate has to be "reasonable and customary" within your region of the country and within your industry for the type of work being performed.   **[Revenue Ruling 73-393]**

So you **cannot** pay your kids $100 an hour for taking out the trash. How do you establish what is "reasonable and customary?" Ask a maid service to come in and give you a written estimate for doing the same work. Then pay your kids a few cents-per-hour less, and you're "home free."   **[IRS Regulation § 1.162-7(a)]**

The kids (as employees) have to document what they did to earn the money, **[Revenue Ruling 73-393]** so have them fill out a simple "work log" with headings like:

It's How Much You KEEP, That Counts! <u>Not</u> how much you <u>Make</u>
Second Edition © 2001

- Date they worked
- Type of work performed
- Amount of time spent working
- Hourly rate you paid them

** PAY ATTENTION HERE ** – This is cool!!!

We're about to show you how to pay for …

- The **car** your high-schooler wants
- Designer-label **clothes** the kids demand
- **Movie and Concert tickets**
- A High School **graduation trip**
- College **tuition**, books and supplies
- Your daughter's expensive **wedding**,
- And lots of other "personal," normally "non-deductible" out-of-pocket expenses,

… <u>ALL in PRE-TAX Dollars!</u>

<u>Here's how you can do it</u> –

The tax-deductible $4,700/year Uncle Sam lets you pay your children as employees, is equivalent to $90.38 per week!

But, you say, "Who gives their kids an $90.38/week allowance?" YOU will now! And here's why…

Let's say you come up with the legal limit of about $90.38 per week worth of home-business related "chores" for them to do. After they turn-in their "work log," you then pay them by check.

So, you'll have to open a separate checking account for them to deposit and cash payroll checks. Of course you'll deposit every week's $90.38 paycheck into that account. Make sure it's an interest-bearing account. (You'll see why in a minute.)

The bank will require it to be a "joint account" with you, since they are *minors*. Although it is technically a "joint" account, only <u>you</u> will be authorized to make withdrawals or to write checks on that account, since the child is a minor.

Reader Alert!
Here's Where It Gets REALLY Interesting!!!

The law requires you to pay them the salary they earned, in order for you to be able to deduct the amount as a business expense.

But the law does not restrict how that money is used after it is paid!   [Revenue Ruling 73-393]

So, you simply tell your child,

> *"I will withdraw $10 (for example) out of each week's pay for you to spend any way you wish, however, the other $80.38 will stay in the (interest-bearing) account to be used by you to pay for your_____."*

Fill in the blank with words like car, graduation trip, wedding, or whatever you like.

Did you ever, in your wildest dreams, anticipate that you would be able to pay for school supplies and tennis shoes, or pay for cars, trips and weddings out of pre-tax dollars? **It's true! It's real! And it's 100% legal!**

There's another practical benefit to this strategy, that's at least as important as the tax benefits. Your child/children will begin learning the value of a dollar. Imagine being at the mall to buy a new pair of shoes. The child has to decide whether he or she wants the $150 designer-label brand or the $45 generic brand – knowing that whatever they have left in their checking/savings account will be theirs someday, to pay for their car, trip, college, wedding, etc.

79

Isn't that a great tax-savings strategy AND a great learning-opportunity for your children?

By the way (in case you are tempted) you cannot charge your dependents for room and board even if they are employees of your home-business, because a parent is legally liable for providing this kind of support for his/her dependent children. Sorry.

[Revenue Ruling 73-393]

Next, Hire Your SPOUSE, So You Can Write-off Medical 'Out-of-Pockets' for YOURSELF!

What? Well, when your spouse is an **employee** of your home-business, he/she is eligible for "benefits" from his/her employer (that's **you**), and those benefits are deductible as business expenses.

[IRS Code § 162(a)]

So you establish <u>this benefit</u> as "company policy:"
> Any and all employees **and their family members** (again, that includes **YOU**) will be reimbursed (by the home-business) for all medical-related expenses not covered under any other insurance plan he/she may have under another employer.

"Any and all employees" means your spouse and your children, "and all members of their family" includes **YOU.**

> **A WORD OF CAUTION:**
> Only establish this company policy if your business will be hiring only your own family members. If you establish this policy and then hire non-family members, you will be required to offer this benefit to them as well, and that could defeat the purpose.

So What Just happened?

You just set-in-place a strategy for legally tax-deducting <u>all</u> annual insurance plan Deductibles, Co-Pays for doctor visits and prescription drugs, and Non-Covered Expenses like braces, glasses, contact lenses, dental work, and possibly even Cosmetic Surgery.

[IRS Regulation 71-588; Plr. 9409006]

No minimum thresholds apply; every single dollar is tax-deductible by the business as an employee benefit cost.

It is important that this "policy" be established in writing, as a legal document. In Appendix C to this book you will find a sample fill-in-the-blanks "Self-Insured Medical Reimbursement Plan," which you may feel free to adopt or adapt, if you wish. **[IRS Regulation 1.105-5(a)]**

A Word About the Level of Your Spouse's Wages

A sole practitioner (Schedule C taxpayer) is not required to pay Unemployment Taxes on the employment of a spouse, however the business IS required to pay Social Security and Medicare payroll taxes on <u>adult</u> family-member employees.

Since those taxes are calculated based on a percentage of the employee's wages, the lower the wage level, the lower the payroll taxes will be. Even if you employ your spouse at "minimum wage," you qualify to use this medical expense reimbursement tax strategy.

[IRS Code § 3306(c)(5); IRS Publication 15, and IRS Circular E all apply]

Pull out a pencil and take a minute now to estimate how much of your kids' expenses could be paid for in pre-tax dollars, and how much of your out-of-pocket medical costs could become business deductions…

Chapter VII

The Key to Your Largest Single
Tax-Deduction May be in Your IGNITION!

Your car, whether you own or lease, probably represents your third-largest monthly expense, coming in right behind withholding taxes and your mortgage or rent.

In all likelihood, however, **your car also represents your largest single source of potential tax-reduction.** So, finding a way to legally write-off a significant portion of your automobile costs, represents a major tax-savings opportunity for you, worth thousands in new, legal tax deductions.

[IRS Temporary Regulations, § 1.274-5T(b)(6)(1)(B)]

You will probably use the same vehicle for both personal use and business use, so the IRS requires that you maintain a vehicle-use log. But that "task" can be reduced to doing just one simple thing each time you slip behind the wheel.

That's right, the record keeping literally takes about as little time as it takes to fasten your seat belt.

You keep a "Vehicle-Use Log" on your dashboard and, each time you get into your car you simply fill in four items:

Date	Destination	Purpose of Trip	Odometer Reading
10/11/01	Local	Sales Calls	00,000
10/12/01	Bank	Bsns deposit	00,000
10/13/01	Post Office	Postage for bsns	00,000

That's it. Destination and Purpose of Trip do not need to be specific. For example, under the heading Destination, you can simply fill in "local travel," and under Business Purpose, you can simply write "sales calls." How long could that take? I'd guess about 5-7 seconds, tops! (See Appendix D to this book for a sample Vehicle-Use Log which you are free to reproduce and use for yourself.)

[IRS Code, § 274(d)]

What about "Commuting Mileage?"

The IRS has ruled that travel from your home to a business destination is tax-deductible **IF** your home qualifies as a "place of business." **[IRS Revenue Ruling 94-47 & 99-7, and IRS Bulletin 1994-29]**

Of course you will have a qualifying home-business, so you will meet the IRS guidelines.

That's easy, you say, but commuting directly from your home to your regular "day job" is **not** tax-deductible, and that's where you put the most miles on your car.

[IRS Code, § 262; Revenue Ruling 90-23, and Internal Revenue Bulletin 1990-11]

That's true, **however**, the IRS's "**Two Business Location Rule**" says that you may deduct the mileage driven "from one business location to a second business location" (i.e., your 'day job').

[Internal Revenue Rulings 55-109 and 99-7, and 1955-1 C.B. 261]

Use this Easy, 4-Step Routine to Meet the IRS Criteria

1. **"Actively engage in your home-business."**
    This can be as simple as placing a business phone call or addressing a business letter first thing each morning, or perform any other "ordinary and necessary" business function before leaving home.

2. **Drive to a "necessary business stop" on the way to your regular "day job." Examples include:**
    - Stop at your Bank branch for a business deposit.
    - Stop to make a sales presentation or to meet a business contact.
    - Stop at the Post Office; get mail from your business P.O. Box.

3. Drive to your "second place of business."

(i.e., Your "regular job."

4. Then reverse the procedure at the end of the day.

That's it! You have just "commuted" to work and back, but rather than the trip being considered a "commute," for tax purposes, your trip now falls under the **"Two Business Location Rule,"** and is legally <u>100% tax-deductible</u>. The deduction was worth 34.5 cents per business-mile in 2001, and is worth 36.5 cents per mile in 2002. Just make sure you are truly conducting business during these brief stops.

Be sure to take all four steps every day possible. Also, be sure to make four entries into your vehicle-use log each day. All of your mileage can be tax-deductible.

A Word of CAUTION:

Some people think (*incorrectly*) that if they conduct home-business activities while at their day job (talk to a co-worker about their MLM business, for example), they can skip steps 1 and 3. Not true. The IRS has ruled, and Tax Courts have confirmed, that if the *primary purpose* of going to the location was to earn a wage, the conduct of your home-business at that location is *secondary*, and thus the trip would be considered to be a *non*-deductible *commute*.

You Get More Than $1,000 in Tax Deductions for Every 3,000 Miles You Drive!

Not taking this deduction is like throwing a $100 bill out your window every time you put 300 miles on your car! Or think of it this way: You could be getting more than $100 in tax deductions for every tank of gas you put in your car.

If you put 12,000 miles on your car commuting each year, following this procedure will make you eligible for more than $4,000 in *new* tax deductions. This procedure is completely legal, and your vehicle-use log will document the deduction to the IRS' satisfaction.

What About Errands and Shopping?

What about shopping trips and other errands? Yes, there are ways to make those miles tax-deductible also. Let's look at a few examples…

Let's say you take your daughter to school each morning and want to legally turn those trips into tax-deductible business mileage. Pick out a bank or post office that is beyond the school to use for your home-business. Each morning drive directly from home to the bank or post office to conduct "business needs." This becomes the primary purpose of the trip. Then, since the school is on your way back to your place of business (home), you might as well drop off your daughter on the way. Since no additional mileage is involved you do not need to record the stop in your Vehicle-Use Log.

Do you make frequent trips to a shopping mall? This one is easy, because you have so many options to use. If there is a quick-copy center in the mall, you could go to the mall to have copies of your business flyers printed. While you're there, you might decide to do some shopping. Of course the shopping would be the secondary purpose of your trip.

In the above example, you could substitute something else for the quick-copy center – getting stamps for your business, buying office supplies, posting flyers on bulletin boards, handing out business cards, etc.

I know a person whose home-business includes selling jewelry from a discount catalog. So when she goes to the mall, she could be "comparison shopping" (checking to see what price local stores are charging for similar items). That's the *primary* business purpose of the trip to the mall, and in her vehicle-use log she would enter Comparison Shopping under the heading labeled Purpose of Trip. If she also does some personal shopping while there, that, of course, is her secondary purpose, so it is not entered into the log.

You have Two Options for Computing Your Business-Vehicle Tax-Deductions

Author's comment: Some of what follow is a little bit tedious, but the deductions are worth thousands of dollars for most people. I suggest you read this section slowly and re-read paragraphs as necessary until you "get it." The examples I provide will help clarify the complicated stuff. It you find this section hard to grasp, just keep good records and let your accountant deal with it at "tax time." ☺

The IRS gives you the option of determining your vehicle deductions by using the "Standard Mileage Rate" (SMR) method or the "Actual Cost" method. **[IRS Proc. 94-73]**

The Easy Option: The **Standard Mileage Rate** method involves simply keeping the vehicle use log as described before. At year-end, add up all of your business miles, and then multiply that number by the IRS Standard Mileage Rate.

The Standard Mileage Rate changes almost every year (34.5 cents per mile for 2001; 36.5 cents per mile for 2002). If you put 10,000 business miles on your car in 2002, you will have $3,700 in vehicle deductions to write-off on your 2002 Tax Return.

The Harder Option: The **Actual Cost Method** requires keeping track of all of your vehicle operating costs, including depreciation or lease payments, insurance, gas, oil, tires, batteries,

89

maintenance and repairs, car washes, automobile club dues, license and registration fees, and interest on your car loan.

If you choose Option 2, here's how to calculate your actual Vehicle Operating Costs:

1. From your vehicle-use log, determine the total number of miles driven for the year.

2. Next, determine how many of those miles were logged as business miles.

3. Now determine the "business use percentage," by dividing the number of business miles by the number of total miles driven.

4. Finally, apply that percentage to the total actual vehicle operating costs for the year, and the resulting figure will be the amount you can write-off on your Tax Return.

For example, if you put 15,000 miles on your car during the year, and 10,000 of those were "business miles," your business use percentage (BUP) would be 66.6%. So you multiply your total actual vehicle operating costs by 0.666, and you will have determined the amount of tax write-off you can claim using the Actual Cost Method.

Usually when something takes more work, it has more value, but that's not necessarily the case here. Believe it or not, most people come out ahead by using the easy SMR option.

The "actual cost" option could be better if you have a gas guzzler, have frequent and expensive repairs and maintenance, drive an exceptionally expensive car, or if you lease your vehicle.

Regardless of which method you select, you can also deduct 100% of parking fees and tolls paid while driving for business purposes.   **[IRS Proc. 90-59, and IRS Bulletin 1990-52 § 4.04]**

And, regardless of which method you select, you can also deduct the business-use percentage of your Vehicle Loan Interest and Personal Property Taxes on your Schedule C.   **[IRS Proc. 95-54 § 5.04]**

BIG Vehicles Can Mean BIGGER Tax Write-Offs!

Some of the most popular SUVs like Chevrolet Suburbans and Ford Excursions are large enough, in terms of gross vehicle weight (GVW), to be exempt from the limitations to expense deductions the IRS imposes on other vehicles under its "luxury auto rules."

These larger vehicles, as "business property," allow you to write-off thousands more on your tax return each year than other vehicles, based on your business use percentage.

You "max-out" at $20,000 in total expense election of all assets for tax year 2001. Just like the SMD, this too is subject to change by Congress each year.

Some "Non-Business" Miles
<u>Also</u> Can be Deducted

Most people elect to use the Standard Mileage Deduction (SMD) method of computing auto deductions due to its simplicity. If you use the SMD method, you can also deduct miles spent doing charitable work, miles going to and from medical appointments, and miles for moving to a new job location.

The rates tend to change frequently, but for year 2002 the mileage deduction allowances are set as follows:

Business Mileage   = **36.5 cents per mile**

[IRS Proclamation 95-54 § 5.01]

Charitable Work   = **14.0 cents per mile**

[IRS Code, § 170(1)]

Medical Care   = **13.0 cents per mile**

[IRS Proclamation 95-54 § 7.02]

Moving/Relocating   = **13.0 cents per mile**

[IRS Proclamation 95-54 § 7.02]

What About Depreciation of Your Car?

Claiming depreciation on the car or truck you use for business purposes has huge tax advantages.

If you use the "actual cost method" your vehicle is considered "Listed Property," and thus is subject to special depreciation rules **if** the business use percentage of your vehicle falls below 50 percent before the end of the "recovery period," which is six years.

[IRS Publication 946, Section 280F]

If this happens, you must re-compute the depreciation using the straight-line method **[IRS Code, § 280F(b)(2)(B)]** and any excess depreciation then becomes taxable income.

[IRS Code, § 280F(b)(1) and 168(g)]

However, if you use the SMD method, depreciation is built into the SMD rate, so you are not affected by the 50% rule just discussed.

This may be another reason to use the much simpler SMD method.

What are the Tax Implications When You Sell or Trade-in Your Automobiles?

First of all, you should consider both financial and tax aspects in making the decision to trade-in or to sell.

When you sell a vehicle, you'll usually get a better net result financially than if you trade-in the vehicle. From a tax standpoint, when you sell the vehicle you will report either a gain or a loss on your tax return for the business portion of the vehicle.

If your decision is to trade-in the vehicle, any gain or loss will be transferred into the "basis" ("cost" for tax purposes) of the new vehicle. In the case of a loss, you will not have the option to declare a loss on your tax return. Simply, your basis in the new vehicle will be adjusted upward accordingly. In the case of a gain, you will defer the gain into the new vehicle by adjusting the basis downward.

To determine whether you will have a gain or loss on the sale of your business vehicle (for tax purposes), you will need to compute the accumulated depreciation that has been taken over the business life of the vehicle. This accumulated depreciation lowers the 'basis' or 'net tax value' on the company records.

For example…

Bill buys a car for $20,000 on January 1, 1997, and uses it 60% for business. The starting business, or "depreciable basis," of the vehicle is $12,000 (60% of $20,000). For simplicity sake, let us assume that the depreciation allowed for 1997, 1998, and 1999 is $2,000 per year. As of 12/31/99 (three years after purchase of the vehicle), the tax basis of the vehicle is reduced to $6,000 ($12,000 starting basis, minus the $6,000 accumulated depreciation).

If Bill sells his car on 12/31/99 for $8,000, he will incur a business loss calculated as follows:

Since the car is used 60% for business, the business portion of the sales price is $4,800 (60% of $8,000). Since the business basis is $6,000, Bill's "business loss" is $1,200. In addition, Bill has a loss on the personal-use portion of the vehicle. However, this loss is **not** tax deductible.

Let's take a look at another scenario...

It is possible that Bill may have been able to trade-in this same vehicle for $12,000 in exchange for a new vehicle with an inflated price and the additional debt or cash obligation for the balance of the new vehicle purchase price.

In this case, Bill would have a "gain" on the disposition of the old vehicle, and that gain would be deferred into the new vehicle by adjusting the basis of the new vehicle.

Since the gain is "carried forward" into the new vehicle, no gain or loss would be reported on Bill's tax return.

Many taxpayers will take the option to calculate vehicle deductions on their tax return by using the 'standard mileage deduction' as indicated earlier. When SMD is used, there is an "implied depreciation" that must be calculated in order to determine if there is a gain or loss on the disposition of the vehicle.

The following table indicates by year the rate to be used to calculate the 'accumulated' depreciation.

That rate has changed 10 times in the past 20 years:

Year	Depreciation Rate
2000-2001	14.0 cents/mile
1994-1999	12.0 cents/mile
1992-1993	11.5 cents/mile
1989-1991	11.0 cents/mile
1988	10.5 cents/mile
1987	10.0 cents/mile
1986	9.0 cents/mile
1983-1985	8.0 cents/mile
1982	7.5 cents/mile
1980-1981	7.0 cents/mile

Using the preceding table, you can compute the basis for the vehicle you are selling or trading, which will determine if the transaction will result in a tax gain or loss on the vehicle.

[IRS Proc. 95-54 § 5.05]

No matter how old your car is, or how many miles you've put on it, a vehicle cannot be depreciated below zero.   If your depreciation gets down to zero, your SMD continues as before, but with <u>none</u> of the deduction allocated to depreciation.   **[IRS Proc. 98-63]**

NOW, Here's How to
Increase Your Vehicle Deductions
by an
ADDITIONAL 50%!

The following is a valuable tax strategy if your family has two vehicles, each worth approximately the same value, and if at least two-thirds the total miles driven (on both cars combined) can qualify as business miles.

For example: You drive 35,000 miles, and 30,000 of those miles qualify as business miles. Your spouse drives 5,000 miles, and none are tax-deductible business miles. The cars are worth about $20,000 each.

- Your total "family miles" equals 40,000 miles (both cars combined).
- 30,000 of those 40,000 miles (75%) are business miles.

If you put all those business miles on one car, you will be limited to the expenses and depreciation limits on one vehicle. The other car will receive no tax deductions, because none of the miles qualify as business miles.

BUT... If you alternate use of the two vehicles, you will still drive 30,000 business miles, but you will put 15,000 of those miles on each of the two cars. Your spouse still drives 5,000 personal miles, but he/she puts 2,500 of those miles on each of the two vehicles.

You may now claim 75% of the miles put on each of the two vehicles, and your vehicle use and depreciation tax-deduction limit increases to $30,000, instead of being capped at $20,000.

This could result in a 50% increase <u>or more</u> in your vehicle deductions!

Chapter VIII

You May Never Take Another Vacation!
From now on, You Could Make Them All
Tax-Deductible Business Trips!

A business based in your home does not need to have any territorial limits. Your customer- or client-prospects may be anywhere in the United States, or North America or even the world.

This means that, wherever you travel **you could be traveling on business,** and reasonable business-travel expenses are tax-deductible, even if tied into personal travel or family vacations! Pay close attention, because the IRS rules about tax-deductibility of business travel are very specific. But they are also very clear, so you should have no problem making sure you are staying within the legal parameters.

The tax law says that anytime your work "requires you to sleep or rest away from your principle place of business" (that's your home), you may deduct reasonable travel and related expenses (such as meals, hotel, rental car, tips, etc.)

[IRS Code, § 162(a)(2) and Revenue Rulings 54-497, 75-432, 63-145, 75-169, 76-453]

The IRS's 3-Part Test

The first step in audit-proofing your business travel deductions is to meet the IRS's '3-Part Test:'

1. The travel must be **usual and customary** within your type of Business.

2. The travel must be conducted with the **intent** to obtain a **direct business benefit**.

3. The travel must be appropriate and helpful to **developing and maintaining** your business.

What's the "51/49% Transportation Rule?"

For travel within the U.S., when you combine business travel with personal or vacation travel, the tax law allows you to **deduct 100% of your transportation costs and lodging...**

- **IF** you spend more than ½ of your days on business, and less than ½ of your days on non-business purposes,

- **AND IF** the primary purpose of your trip was business. (Of course, you are the one who determines whether the primary purpose of your trip was business or pleasure.

[IRS Code, § 1.162-2(b)(2)]

What is Considered a 'Business Day?'

Depending upon the method of travel and the length of the trip, getting to and from your destination can take up the majority of a day (or more) each way. Therefore, it is important to know how the IRS defines "business day" which we will cover shortly.

If the primary purpose of your travel is business, the cost of transporting yourself to your "business destination" is tax deductible, whether you travel First Class air, Coach Class air, train, car, boat or even chartered plane.

Once you arrive at your destination, you will incur certain other expenses, such as taxi fare, car rental, hotel, meals, tips, etc.

You may deduct food and lodging expenses for 'business days' even if your trip does not include enough business days for it to qualify as a "business trip." For example, if you make a 5 day trip, but only 2 days are spent on business, you may deduct your meals and hotel for those two days only, but you may not claim any of the transportation costs, because the trip will not have met the 51/49% Transportation Rule discussed earlier.

What About Weekends and Holidays?

If weekend days and/or holidays fall between business days, they are considered by the IRS to be business days. For example, you travel to a destination on Wednesday, do business on Thursday and Friday, and do business again on Tuesday. Saturday and Sunday will be considered to be business days and Monday considered a personal day.

The test is this: Would it be practical to return home for the weekend or holiday days? If so, they are not deductible. But if it would not be practical to return home (due to the expense or the time required), they are considered to be business days, regardless of what you actually do on those days. **[IRS Regulations, § 1.274-4(d)(2)(v)]**

What About Saturday Night Stay-Overs?

Oftentimes, airlines offer substantial fare discounts if a Saturday night stay is included.

Good news for you! **The government actually used common sense in making a determination about this one.**

"If a substantial discount is available by including a Saturday night stay, Saturday may be considered a (tax-deductible) business travel day and Sunday is considered a (tax-deductible) business stay-over day" even if you return home on Monday.   **[PLR 9237014]**

When is a Travel Day Also a Business Day?

Even if you conduct no business on the day you travel, it is still a tax-deductible business day **IF** you spend at least four hours in travel. That four hours includes the time it takes you to get to the airport, park, check-in, wait for the plane, fly, disembark, wait for your luggage, get a taxi or rental car and get to your hotel.

[IRS Regulations, § 1.274-4(d)(2)(i)]

As inefficient as airline transportation is these days, just about any trip you take could qualify under these criteria.

So, if getting to and from your destination takes four hours or more, the entire day qualifies as a "business day."

Does It Make Any Difference
What Method of Transportation I Use?

Simple answer: No. If you travel by auto, airplane, train, boat or motorcycle, your actual travel expenses are 100% fully deductible if the trip qualifies as "business travel." **[IRS Publication 463]**

Can I Claim my Spouse's Expenses if
he/she Accompanies Me to a
Business Meeting or Convention?

Expenses of an accompanying spouse are deductible **only if**:

- His/her travel is for a bona fide business purpose (i.e., not just accompanying you),

- He or she is an employee of the business (see Chapter VI), and

- The travel and related expenses would be deductible for him/her even if he/she were making the trip alone.

[IRS Code, § 274(m)(3)]

Special Note: Taking the kids along tends to make the IRS think of the travel as a personal vacation trip, **so make sure the kids also are employees of your business** and that they also have a bona fide business purpose for attending the meeting or convention.

Can I Deduct Laundry & Dry Cleaning?

Yes, if you are required to remain out-of-town for one or more nights, you can deduct the cost of laundering or dry cleaning any clothing required for that trip, **even if you wait and have the cleaning done after you return home**.

[Internal Revenue Ruling 63-145 and 1963-2 C.B. 86]

Let's Summarize the Deductions for Traveling on Business

"Ordinary and Necessary" business expenses include:

- 50% of the cost of all meals,
  [IRS Regulations, § 1.162-2(a)]

- 100% of transportation and lodging,
  [IRS Publication 463]

- 100% of laundry and dry cleaning of clothing used during business portion of trip,
  [Internal Revenue Ruling 63-145 and 1963-2 C.B. 86]

- Telephone calls, both local and long distance,
  [IRS Regulations, § 1.162-2(a)]

- Local transportation from airport to hotel, to customer visits, and back to airport (including taxis, limos, trains, buses, rental cars, etc. [IRS Publication 463]

- All appropriate tips associated with otherwise-deductible expenses. [IRS Publication 463]

Keeping Audit-Proof
Business-Trip Records is Easy

This is not difficult unless you procrastinate and "do it later."

All the IRS requires is the answers to 5 questions:

1. **<u>WHERE</u> DID THE MONEY GO?**
   List each individual expenditure, such as plane tickets, taxi fares, meals (listed separately), tips, registration fees, etc.

2. **<u>WHEN</u> DID YOU SPEND IT?**
   Dates and times of departure and return, as well as date of each expenditure.

3. **<u>WHERE</u> DID YOU SPEND IT?**
   City you flew to, restaurant you ate in, from-and-to of each taxi fare, name of hotel you stayed in, who you gave tips to, etc.

4. **<u>WHY</u> DID YOU SPEND IT?**
   Justify the business purpose of the trip itself, and the business reason for each expenditure. Not everything is automatically deductible. For example, in-room hotel movie rentals and purchases from a hotel room mini-bar are normally not deductible.

5. **<u>CAN YOU PROVE</u> YOU <u>PAID YOUR BILLS?</u>**
   You'll need copies of paid receipts for hotel stays, transportation expenses, conference fees, and any individual expenditure of $75 or more.

Personally, I even get a receipt for buying the morning paper, because I've developed a habit of getting a receipt every time I buy anything. It's a lot easier to throw away a receipt you end up not needing, than to try to justify an expense without one.

Here's How to Turn this 'Chore' Into a Simple 'Habit'

1. Carry a small spiral-bound notebook in your pocket, with a pen attached and a paper-clip on the back cover.

2. Every time you spend a penny on anything (even non-deductible expenses) record it in your notebook and clip the receipt inside the back cover.

3. Each evening, review your notebook to make sure everything you wrote in your notebook is clearly legible, and write notes on your receipts to remind you three years from now what each receipt was for.

4. Staple or paper-clip that day's receipts together, and put them in a safe place, like your suitcase or briefcase.

5. Start a new page in your notebook for each new day.

Can you see how making this a "habit" can turn a "chore" into a "no-brainer?"

107

If you would be interested in learning how to obtain Tax Audit "insurance," on-call Legal Services, Credit Repair or Investment Planning advice, please email us at <u>Info@HomeBusinessTaxSavings.com</u> and we will send you free information.

Chapter IX

Meals & Entertainment
Can be Legally Deductible too!

The IRS lumps-together the broad categories of Entertainment, Business Meals, Business-Related Sports, Recreation and Amusement under the tax heading "Entertainment."

Be Aware of the 50% Rule!

There is one significant difference between tax-deductible entertainment expenses and nearly all other tax-deductible business expenses: When you have qualifying entertainment expenses, they generally are deductible at only 50% of their actual cost.

This change to the tax law was passed by Congress in 1994 to discourage abuse of this deduction and the "three-martini lunch."

Here's How to Determine Whether
Entertainment IS or is NOT
Legally Deductible...

There are only three terms you must be familiar with:

1. Four-Requirement Test
2. Clear Business Setting
3. Associated Entertainment.

1. "The Four-Requirement Test"

If you meet all four steps of the **Four-Requirement Test** you probably have a qualifying business entertainment expense.

The Four Requirements are:

- At the time you committed to spend the money, you had more than a general expectation of future business benefit.
- During the entertainment, you actively discussed the topic that could produce future business benefit.
- Your principal reason for engaging in the activity was to actively conduct business.
- You incurred the expense to speak with the person who produced your expectation of future business benefit.

2. "Clear Business Setting"

It is not necessary to meet those four requirements if your expenses took place in a **Clear Business Setting**. The IRS has a definition for that, of course.

It says that entertainment occurs in a **Clear Business Setting** when:

- The person you are entertaining knows that you are spending money on him/her in order to directly attempt to further your business interests.

- You spend money on a hospitality suite at a convention where you display products to further your business.

- You have no meaningful social or personal relationship with the person or people you are entertaining.

The IRS considers restaurants, your home, hotel meeting rooms and hotel dining rooms to be "conducive to business discussion without significant distraction." Thus, business entertainment taking place in these locations are deemed to be in a "clear business setting."

Locations the IRS tend to question, relative to "clear business setting," include night clubs, theaters, sporting events and stage shows, because these locations all have distractions that make it unlikely that significant business discussion can take place.

However, although expenses in those settings may <u>not</u> be deductible under the "Clear Business Setting" rule, they may very well qualify under the "Associated Entertainment" Rule.

3. "Associated Entertainment"

The IRS says that **"Associated Entertainment"** is entertainment that is <u>not directly</u> related to the conduct of business, but <u>IS in</u>directly associated with conduct of business.

For example, entertainment that immediately precedes or follows active conduct of business may be considered "associated entertainment."

Let's say you take prospective clients to the theater and then directly after the event, you take them to dinner and have (to use IRS terminology) a "substantial and bona fide business discussion." The dinner expense falls under Clear Business Setting and the theater expense falls under Associated Entertainment, so both would be deductible at 50% of their actual cost.

Do you regularly go out to lunch with business associates or colleagues? Depending upon the type of home-business you run, business associates might be among your best prospects.

If you 'talk business' at lunch, and if they are casual acquaintances (not close friends), you may be eligible to deduct 50% of the cost of your meal. Or you could "pick up their tab" and deduct

50% of both meals. They'll get a free meal, but you'll only spend about the same as you would have spent anyway.

Yes, Even GOLF Can be Deductible
(as can some other sporting activities)

Are you a golfer? Want to deduct greens fees and/or meals in the golf club's dining room or grill? Golf is one participation sport that can qualify under the Four Requirements Rule. Of course you cannot play golf with the same people every week and still qualify, but if you're the type of person who likes to take prospects to the club with you, or who likes to call or drop-by the golf course and ask the starter to put you in a twosome or threesome, this is ideal.

Unlike most other sports, golf offers ample opportunity to "hold substantial business discussions" while walking or riding down the fairway, while waiting on the tee for the foursome ahead to putt-out, or while waiting for a fellow player across the fairway to hit his or her shot.

Other activities that might be treated similarly, depending on the circumstances, include sailing, fishing and hunting. And you can probably think of others as well.

Documenting Business-Entertainment Expenses is Not Difficult

The simplest way to document your tax-deductible entertainment expenses is to get a receipt for everything, staple related receipts together, and write, in ink, directly on the receipt (within 24 hours, according to the IRS),

- **The <u>Date</u> the expense was incurred.**
  Generally this means the date of the entertainment itself (i.e., if you purchased season tickets to a sporting event to entertain clients and prospects, you would record the date, etc., of each individual event, as it occurred).
  [IRS Regulation 1.274-5(b)(3)(ii)]

- **The <u>Amount</u> of the expense.**
  The numbers imprinted on the front of the receipt can fade over time, becoming illegible, so write the Amount on the receipt in ink.
  [IRS Regulations1.274-2(b)(1)(i) and Reg. 1.274-5T(c)(2)(iii)(B)]

- **The <u>Place</u> the expense was incurred.**
  Name and location of the venue, as well as the type of event, if not obvious. List the place of the business discussion if the event was "Associated Entertainment."
  [IRS Regulation 1.274-5(b)(3)(iii)]

- **Your <u>Purpose</u> for incurring the expense.**
  Be sure to relate your "why" to your business, of course. Why are you entertaining this particular person, and what business result do you expect to come about as a result?
  [IRS Regulation 1.274-5(b)(3)(iv)]

- **The <u>Relationship</u> to you of the person(s) you entertained**
  or job title, and other relevant information that explains
  why you entertained that particular person.

[IRS Regulation 1.274-5(b)(3)(v)]

A Word of CAUTION:

There is an IRS requirement that this documentation be recorded within 24 hours of incurring the entertainment expense, so it is a good habit to do this as soon as you return to your home, office or hotel.

Want a Professional Recommendation? <u>Be Conservative</u>!

"Deductible Entertainment" is a tricky area of tax law and it is not the area where most people will get their greatest tax breaks. So most people should be conservative and use good judgment when deciding to take entertainment expense deductions.

But if your own circumstances are such that you could derive large tax savings in this category, be sure to obtain good tax advice from someone highly experienced in home-business tax law.

And be sure to obtain that advice before you incur the expenses, because oftentimes making just a minor adjustment can turn a non-deductible expense into a deductible one.

NOTE: Tax Court Rulings are continually providing clarification about what does and what does not qualify as a business-entertainment deduction, so you need to keep up-to-date with changes. By owning this book you qualify for a FREE email subscription to "Tax Tips You Can Count On." See page 203 to learn how to subscribe to this valuable free service.

Chapter X

Don't dread that dreaded word, DOCUMENTATION

We learned in Chapter VII how simple it is to keep vehicle-use records, in Chapter VIII how to keep business travel records, and in Chapter X how to keep easy documentation that meet all the requirements of the IRS.

Here's more good news! Documentation of day-to-day expenses is equally easy. Start by setting up and labeling 9 file folders or 9 shoe boxes or 9 slots in an accordion file to hold your receipts. **Here Are Your 9 Labels** and what goes into each of them:

ADVERTISING and PROMOTION

(These expenses relate to line 8 of Schedule C)

Into this folder, place documentation for:

- **Paid Advertising**: classifieds, radio spots, etc.
- **Mailing List Rental Fees & Biz-Op Lists.**
- **Direct-Mail Costs**: postage, envelopes, printing.
- **Promotional Materials**: prospecting tapes, videos, flyers.

<u>NOTE:</u> Attach evidence of payment (such as cancelled check) to each invoice.

<u>Author's Note:</u> The IRS only requires Receipts and Proof-of-Payment, but I prefer to attach to each receipt, a copy of the advertisement or promotional piece.

118

VEHICLE OPERATING COSTS
(These expenses relate to lines 10 and 20 of Schedule C)

Into this folder, place documentation for:

- **Vehicle-Use Log** (see Chapter VII and Appendix)
- **Gas, Toll and Parking** receipts
- **Maintenance and Repair records**
- **Purchase/Lease Monthly Payments**
- **Interest, Taxes, Fees and Insurance paid**

<u>**NOTE**</u>: Attach evidence of payment (such as cancelled check) to each invoice.

LEASE/PURCHASE of BUSINESS ASSETS
(These expenses relate to lines 13 and 20 of Schedule C)

Into this folder, place documentation for lease or purchase of business assets such as:

Computers	**Fax Machines**	**Scanners**
Phone Systems	**Beepers**	**Pagers**
Furniture	**Furnishings**	**TV/VCR**
Cell Phones	**Tape Duplication System**	

<u>**NOTE**</u>: Attach evidence of payment (such as cancelled check) to each invoice/pmt.

WAGES, COMMISSIONS & EMPLOYEE BENEFITS PAID

(These expenses relate to lines 14, 19 and 26 of Schedule C)

Into this folder, place documentation for:

- **Wages Paid to Family-Member Employees**
- **Time-Sheets or Work-Logs**
- **Employment Contracts**
- **Evidence that wage-rates paid were "reasonable."**
- **Copies of Payroll Tax Forms and Payroll Reports**
- **Commissions Paid to others, if applicable**
- **Costs of Medical Reimbursement benefit**

NOTE: Attach evidence of payment (such as cancelled check) to each invoice.

LEGAL & PROFESSIONAL FEES & COSTS

(These expenses relate to line 17 of Schedule C)

Into this folder, place documentation for:

- **Legal Fees**
- **Tax Preparation and Tax Advice**
- **Outside Bookkeeping or Payroll Services**
- **Purchase of This Book!!!**

NOTE: Attach evidence of payment (such as cancelled check) to each invoice.

BUSINESS USE OF HOME

(These expenses relate to line 18 of Schedule C)

Into this folder, place documentation for:

- **Calculations to Determine Business Use Percentage**
- **Mortgage or Rent payments**
- **Utility bills**
- **Phone Bills**
- **Receipts for lawn care, house cleaning service, etc.**
- **Home Repairs, Maintenance and Improvements**
- **Costs of Internet Access, Cell Phones & Pagers**
- **Alarm System**

NOTE: It is easier to justify all of the above if you have a floor-plan of your home, indicating the Business Use of each room, and/or photos that show the Business Use of the rooms you are including in your Business Use Percentage (BUP) calculations. Attach evidence of payment (such as cancelled check) to each invoice.

OFFICE SUPPLIES

(These expenses relate to line 22 of Schedule C)

Into this folder, place documentation for:

Stationery	**Business Cards**	**Address Labels**
Fax paper	**Calendars**	**File folders Mailing Boxes**
Desk supplies		**Cleaning Supply's**

Everything from Pencils to Toner Cartridges!

NOTE: Even business equipment and other "assets" can be considered "supplies" if their purchase cost is only a few hundred dollars or less. Attach evidence of payment (such as cancelled check) to each invoice.

123

BUSINESS TRAVEL & ENTERTAINMENT
(These expenses relate to line 24 of Schedule C)

Into this folder, place documentation for
Everything covered in Chapters VIII and IX, including…

Air fare receipt (with date and time of departure & arrival written on it)
> *Remember, spending 4 hours in transit counts as a Business Day*

Receipts for all expenditures in excess of $75.00
Notes on all individual expenditures less than $75.00
Record of number of hours of business activity and personal time each day
Hotel receipts (with any Personal expenses annotated and deducted)
Entertainment receipts, with required annotations.

NOTE: Attach evidence of payment (such as cancelled check) to each invoice.

MISC. OTHER BUSINESS EXPENSES
Use this folder for:
- **Bank statements**
- **Business license, fees or taxes**
- **Repairs to business equipment**
- **Interest paid on business loans**
- **Interest and fees paid on *business* credit cards**
- **Banking fees**
- **Postage and delivery fees**
- **Homeowners or renters insurance**
- **Mortgage interest paid**
- **Real estate taxes**
- **Dues and subscriptions**
- ***And anything else that might possibly be deductible.***

NOTE: Attach evidence of payment (such as cancelled check) to each invoice.

If your home-business is an MLM, everyone in your downline, upline and crossline, needs this book, right? You could earn "referral commissions" through our generous Affiliate Program. Get full details by visiting our web site at **www.HomeBusinessTaxSavings.com**

A Very Important Note About
Record-Keeping

Most people <u>do</u> know that they need to keep copies of invoices or bills to document their tax-deductible expenses.

But many people do <u>not</u> know that they also are required by the IRS to be able to prove they <u>paid</u> those invoices/bills. Proof of payment IS a requirement for making those expenses deductible. Here's why and how…

The logic is not difficult to understand: A taxpayer could order a $5,000 piece of business equipment, receive an invoice for it, but then return the item for a full refund. If the IRS only required the invoice for documentation, the taxpayer could claim a $5,000 deduction for a piece of equipment he/she never kept or paid for.

Therefore, the IRS requires the taxpayer to provide proof of the <u>cost</u> of the item (invoice) **and** proof that it was **paid**.

That proof could be in the form of a 'PAID" stamp on the invoice, if the item was paid for in cash. Or it could be documented with a cancelled business check. (If your bank provides only copies of your checks, be sure you have a copy of both sides of the check!)

127

If you pay by charge card for a tax-deductible item, the IRS considers the item to have been paid for when the charge card company records the charge (i.e., December charges are included in the tax-year ending in December, even though you will not receive the statement until January).

Therefore, your proof-of-payment documentation should include a copy of your charge card receipt (the "flimsy") or a copy of your monthly invoice, which lists the charge on it.

Keeping a daily appointment calendar and recording expenses on it is accepted by the IRS as proof of expenditures below a certain number ($75 for travel related expenses, for example).

Chapter XI

Easy Steps to
Audit-Proofing Your Taxes

When most taxpayers hear the word "audit" they get the same feeling as when they look into their rear-view mirror and see flashing blue lights behind them.

So first, let's put "audit" into perspective.

An audit it nothing more than the IRS's attempt to see if you reported all of your income accurately and if you qualified for all of the deductions you claimed.

If you are driving 65 mph in a 65 mph zone, you have nothing to fear if a highway patrolman uses radar to check your speed, right? Well, likewise, if all of the deductions you are claiming on your Tax Returns are legal and adequately documented, there's no reason to fear an audit.

Maintaining the documentation the IRS looks for does not have to be time consuming, does not require an accountant, and is easy.

These are the <u>**5 Most Important Steps**</u> every taxpayer should take to Audit-Proof their taxes...

1. When documenting deductions, the IRS requires that you produce evidence that you incurred the expense, which is usually going to be a copy of your invoice. **But** they **also require proof that you paid the invoice, so keep your cancelled checks attached to your invoices** for all expenses you are deducting on your Tax Return. (By the way, when a bill is charged to a credit card, it is deemed to have been paid when the card charge is incurred, so keep credit card statements also.)

2. Many people keep a separate checking account for their business income and expenses, which is generally a good idea. But you must know that **the IRS will consider all deposits into that account as representing "earned income."** If they add up your deposits and come up with a different number from what you reported, it may look like you under-reported your income. (That's not a good thing!) Perhaps some of your deposits were personal funds you were <u>loaning</u> your company so that you could buy promotional materials. Solution: **Mark clearly in your checkbook register the source of every deposit into your business account.**

3. If you hire your children and/or spouse so that the expenses are deductible, **pay them by check, and require them to document what they did** to earn each check. For example, they could turn in monthly or weekly calendar pages or timesheets on which they've recorded the work they did, what days they did it on, and the number of hours worked. (Ex.: 18th, Mowed Lawn, 3 hours). You may also be required to **show that the amount you are paying your family members is "reasonable."** So get a professional lawn care company to give you a written estimate for mowing your lawn, and then pay your family member approximately that amount. Do the same with a maid service if your kids are going to do housecleaning for wages, for example.

4. If your Schedule C at the end of the year shows your home-based business with a net loss for the year, an auditor may require you to prove that you intended to make a profit. Profit-intent is required to prove that you are in a legitimate business, and the IRS will accept a Business Plan as an important part of your proof. **So have a Business Plan!** (We've provided you a draft in Appendix F of this book.)

5. **Never attend a tax-audit in person** (see next section).

Get a tax lawyer or accountant who is an Enrolled Agent to attend in your place. EA's are authorized to represent clients in tax audits. If you are present, the auditor may ask trick questions, hoping you'll slip up somewhere. But if you're not there, they can't ask you.

Your chances of an Audit are slim, but if you follow these five steps, you'll have nothing to fear.

NEVER Appear In-Person for a Tax Audit!

You **never** want to show up **in person** for a tax audit! **Never, never, NEVER!** Always have an Enrolled Agent, CPA or other IRS-approved representative appear in your place.

An Enrolled Agent is someone authorized by the IRS to represent clients at IRS Audits and Audit-Appeals. Many Enrolled Agents are former IRS agents themselves, so they really know what an audit is all about!

If you are **not** personally present, you cannot answer questions about "apparent discrepancies" – questions that may cause you to answer inaccurately, simply due to vague recollections of something that occurred three years prior.

For example, the auditor says, "Your appointment calendar says you were in Denver on this date, but you have claimed an entertainment expense for Chicago on that same date."

If **you** are present, you'll be expected to have a good answer. But if your **agent** is present **instead** of you, he or she simply says, "Obviously the Denver trip got cancelled or postponed."

Please DO use the 9 file folders! The "old trick" of showing up at an audit with a basketful of receipts is no longer tolerated by the IRS.

"Nothing to Fear but Fear Itself"

If you keep all receipts, and keep them grouped by category, and use those receipts to have your taxes prepared, **you have nothing to fear, even if you receive an audit notice**.

If all the deductions you claimed are legal, and if you've kept necessary documentation (both of which are described in this book), an audit of your Tax Return will simply be an "unavoidable inconvenience."

But it will <u>not</u> be something to be feared!

An Audit Can Actually be a Good Thing --- *Really!*

On average, your chances of being randomly audited is about 0.5%. That's ½ of 1 percent. One chance out of every 200 taxpayers. In fact, in 1999 only 1 out of every 318 tax returns were audited.

But if you <u>are</u> audited and you've followed the rules and have the documentation, there's nothing for the IRS to "find." So, here's the good news about having been audited…

The law says that if, during the conduct of a routine audit, the IRS does not find any "evidence of intentional fraud" (*which they obviously won't in your case*) then they are not allowed to perform another routine audit of your returns again for at least three more years, even if your name again comes up in the computer-generated random list of returns to be audited.

So, audits are rare, but they do happen. But "if you're driving within the speed limit, there's no reason to fear a radar gun."

Bottom-line on Audits:

- Follow the tax law.

- Keep required documentation.

- Put your audit in the hands of an Enrolled Agent or CPA.

One of the greatest advantages of having a home-business is that it ends up increasing your take-home pay by some 10% (+/-).

Essentially that means that Uncle Sam is <u>paying</u> the cost of running your home-based business. How could your possibly lose?

You can't!

Check it out in the next chapter…

136

Chapter XII

How to Add
Hundreds of Dollars Every Month
To Your Take-Home Pay!

Do you remember your first day on the job, when you had to fill out all sorts of paperwork? One of those papers was a W-4 Tax Withholding Form, on which you determined the "number of allowances you are claiming."

That number, coupled with your answer to whether your filing status is Single or Married, told your employer what percentage of your money he or she is required to withhold from your wages for various Federal and State taxes.

Three Common Misunderstandings
About W-4 Forms

The FIRST Misconception most people have about W-4s:

The term "Allowances" has nothing to do with the number of people in your household. **Allowances do not mean Dependents**. It is simply a term representing the inverse of the percentage of your wages to be withheld.

137

For example, if you claim three Allowances, a certain percentage of your wages will be withheld for taxes. Now if you file a revised W-4 with your employer, doubling the number of Allowances you are claiming to six, much less money will be withheld from each paycheck.

SECOND Misconception most people have about W-4s:

Most people do not understand the purpose of withholding taxes. If you've ever owned a home, you probably understand the term "escrow." It means that, with each month's house payment, the mortgage company is also collecting $1/12^{th}$ of your annual Property Taxes. That way, when the tax bill comes in, your mortgage company has the money to pay it for you. Assuming your property tax amount does not change mid-year, when the bill comes in the mortgage company will have "in your escrow account," exactly the amount needed to pay it off.

Withholding taxes work exactly the same way. The number of Allowances you put on your W-4, tells your employer how much you expect to owe in Income Taxes during the course of the year. The employer, then deducts a *pro rata* amount from each paycheck.

138

To use round numbers, let's say you expect to pay $12,000 in Income Taxes this year. If you get paid once a month, your employer will withhold $1,000 from each of your 12 monthly paychecks. If you get paid twice a month, your employer will withhold $500 out of each of your 24 paychecks. If you get paid weekly, your employer will withhold $1/52^{nd}$ of $12,000 from each paycheck.

In each case, the amount withheld during the course of the entire year, should come out to exactly what you owe in taxes. If your number of Allowances was computed accurately, at the end of the year you will owe no additional taxes, and you will get no tax refund. That's the way is should be.

If your withholding wasn't high enough, you'll end up owing the Government additional taxes at the end of the year. If you've had too much withheld, you'll end up getting a refund at the end of the year.

Contrary to popular opinion, a Refund is not a good_thing! Getting a refund at the end of the year, means that you have given Uncle Sam an interest-free loan for a full year. If, for example, you get back $2,400 in Tax Refunds, most people would be excited. BUT what that really means is that $200 cash that you could have put into your own pocket every single month, you gave, instead, to the government as an interest-free loan.

139

Pardon my bluntness, but that's stupid. If that's the only way you can save money, then give the money to me. I'll invest it and earn interest on it, and give the principal back to you next April 15th, but I'll keep the interest. That's the same thing you're letting Uncle Sam do!

The THIRD Misconception most people have about W-4s:

Many people believe that, if they claim a high number of Allowances on their W-4, they're more likely to get audited. I've been assured by former top IRS executives that that just is not true, as long as the number of allowances is appropriate. In other words, if you <u>were</u> claiming <u>4</u> Allowances, and then changed your W-4 to claim 12 Allowances, and then, at the end of the year, you ended up owing $3,000 in additional Income Taxes... well... let's just say that's not a good thing.

The trick is to make the amount of money withheld from your paycheck come out to almost exactly what your annual tax obligation will be, and in a few minutes we'll show you how to do that.

Now that Your Deductions are Going UP ▲
-Thanks to your home-based business-
Your Withholding Taxes Can Go DOWN ▼

Nationwide, the average amount of withholding is more than 30%, meaning about one-third of the money you earn gets gobbled up for various taxes, and then you get what's left, in a check called your "take-home pay."

THIS IS IMPORTANT! You're about to learn how to increase your take-home pay by as much as 10 percent or more, easily, legally and quickly, **usually starting with your very next paycheck!**

As we've said, in theory, the amount of money withheld during the course of the year should match the amount you owe at the end of the year. If this happens, you owe no additional taxes and you get no refund at the end of the year.

If too little was withheld, you end up having to send in a check with your Tax Return. If too much was withheld, you file for a Refund, which we've explained is not a good thing!

With a **qualifying home-business and using the deductions described in this book**, you are now going to begin paying a **lot less in taxes** than you did before you learned about all these home-business deductions. There is a formula for forecasting how much

141

your taxes will go down, based on how much of your home is used in your business, how many business miles you will put on your car, the number of business trips (formerly called *vacations*) you will anticipate taking, etc.

Anyone can submit a revised W-4 at any time. Once you know how much you will be saving on taxes, you simply go to your payroll office and fill out a new W-4, claiming a higher number of allowances.

Your new W-4 will result in your employer withholding far less from your wages, thus, your take-home pay goes up. That increase should show up in your very next paycheck.

The home-business tax deductions explained in this book could allow most people to claim 4 to 6 allowances, and sometimes the number can be as high as 8-9, or even higher in some cases.

Remember: Do not confuse "allowances" with "deductions" or "dependents." Allowances have nothing to do with the number of people in your household.

The result? Roughly speaking, for every $1,000 in your current paycheck, you'll have an additional $100 (could be more, could be

142

less) in all <u>future</u> paychecks, after you've filed a new W-4 with your employer.

Many people find that their take-home pay increases by $200 to $500 per month or more!   That's like giving yourself a "pay-raise."

How big will YOUR increase in take home pay be?

Let's take a look!

If you had a home-based business at any time in the past 3 years, and if anything in this book is new to you, you probably missed out on a lot of legal deductions you could have taken, had you known about the deductions described in this book.

The law allows you up to 3 years to file Amended Returns to claim the deductions you missed. For details, email your request to **Info@HomeBusinessTaxSavings.com**.

W-4 Allowance Worksheet for a Taxpayer with a Home-Based Business

Every wage-earning employee is required, by law, to have a Form W-4 on file with their employer's payroll office. The IRS Code, §3402, authorizes employees to adjust the number of Allowances claimed on their W-4 any time a change in circumstances suggests that their income tax liability will significantly alter. Your employer is required to allow you to change your W-4 at any time, and is required to immediately adjust your withholding in accordance with the number of Allowances you claim on your Revised W-4. That normally means you will see the change in your very next paycheck, unless you submitted a revised W-4 just immediately before a payday, in which case the change may be delayed until the following payday. **Computing the approximate number of allowances to claim on your W-4, is a 2 Part process.**

PART 1:

1. Look at the Form W-4 supplied in Appendix E. Following instructions contained in the center section of Form W-4, compute the correct number for Line H, and write that number here: _____ **Allowances**

PART 2:

1. a. How many business miles will you put on your car(s) during a 12 month period?_____ miles
    b. Multiply this number of miles times 0.345, and record the answer here: $ _____

2. a. Will you employ your spouse in your business? YES or NO
    b. If YES, how much out-of-pocket does your family spend on non-reimbursed medical costs? $ _____

3. a. Will you employ your child(ren) in your business? YES or NO
    b. If YES, multiply [Number of children to be hired] X [Amount each will be paid per year]: $ _____

4. a. Will you take any Business Trips this year? YES or NO
    b. If YES, Approximate total travel costs (including your employees): $ _____

5. Out-of-Pocket expenses for advertising, supplies, monthly fees/dues, 50% of meals/ent., etc. $ _____

6. Total deductions for equipment, furniture and fixtures (see Chapter V) $ _____

7. Total items 1 – 6, and write the result here: $ _____

8. Anticipated total revenue this year from your home-business only: $ _____

9. Subtract the Amount appearing on Line 7 from that Appearing on Line 6, and record the result: $ _____

10. a. If your total annual income from all sources is under $53,000 (Married) or
    under $31,000 (Single), Divide the Amount on Line 8 $_____ by $4,400 = _____ **Allowances**

    -OR-   **-OR-**

    b. If your total annual income from all sources is over $53,000 (Married) or
    over $31,000 (Single), Divide the Amount on Line 8 $_____ by $2,400 = _____ **Allowances**

NOW,

    Add the number you arrived at in Part 1: _____ Allowances
    And the number you arrived at in Part 2 (a or b) + _____ Allowances

---

This Sum goes on line 5 of your NEW Form W-4   = _____ *Allowances*

NOTES:
*   **If your total exceeds 10, consider limiting claim to 10, and claiming the balance of your refund when you file your tax return; claiming 11+ allowances on your W-4 requires your employer to obtain IRS approval.**
*   **The above calculations are estimates only and may not be accurate for all taxpayers in all situations if you have other income or deductions.**
*   **Taxpayers should consult a qualified home-business tax professional for assistance with W-4 allowance calculations, and calculations should be reviewed regularly to insure that you will not owe taxes when you file your tax return.**

It's How Much You KEEP, That Counts! Not how much you Make
Second Edition © 2001

This book makes a great *tax-deductible* "business gift." For information about buying multiple copies at a discount, email **Info@HomeBusinessTaxSavings.com**.

Take-Home Pay Increase Estimator

Directions:

1. Locate your approximate *monthly* wages in the left-hand column of the table below that applies to you.

2. What number did you come up with in Step 10 on the previous page? Look for that number across the top of the appropriate table below.

3. Where those two numbers intersect, you'll see the *approximate* amount of your take-home pay increase.

MARRIED PERSONS FILING *JOINT* RETURNS
Additional Take-home Pay Due to Home-Business

Gross Wages (Monthly)	Additional Allowances Due to Home-Business			
	4	6	8	9
$1,000	$ 72	$ 72	$ 72	$ 72
$1,500	$137	$144	$144	$144
$2,000	$137	$206	$222	$222
$2,500	$137	$206	$275	$294
$3,000	$137	$206	$275	$309
$3,500	$137	$206	$275	$309
$4,000	$145	$413	$283	$317
$4,500	$210	$279	$348	$382
$5,000	$256	$344	$413	$447

SINGLE PERSONS and MARRIEDS FILING *SEPARATELY*
Additional Take-home Pay Due to Home-Business

Gross Wages (Monthly)	Additional Allowances Due to Home-Business			
	4	6	8	9
$1,000	$120	$120	$120	$120
$1,500	$138	$192	$192	$192
$2,000	$138	$206	$270	$270
$2,500	$167	$235	$304	$338
$3,000	$234	$302	$371	$406
$3,500	$256	$364	$433	$468
$4,000	$256	$384	$501	$536
$4,500	$256	$384	$512	$578
$5,000	$256	$384	$512	$582

NOTE: The above calculations are estimates only and may not be accurate for all taxpayers in all situations. Taxpayers should consult a tax professional for assistance with W-4 allowance calculations.

It's How Much You KEEP, That Counts! Not how much you Make
Second Edition © 2001

See page 203 to sign up to receive FREE tax-law updates and useful tax-savings tips via our free email letter, *Tax Tips You Can Bank On.*

Chapter XIII

Putting It All Together

What have we learned, and what does it mean --
to YOU?

First, we've learned that America has two tax systems, and either you've been in the wrong one or you've been in the right one, but not getting all the tax-reduction benefits you qualified for.

Either way, you will no longer lose out on legitimate tax breaks just because no one ever told you about them.

Before you read this book, if I had asked you, "Who in America gets the most tax breaks?" what would you have replied?   Most people would have said, "The wealthy people who can afford good tax lawyers to find them all the loopholes."

But that really isn't true, is it? It is people who establish and run a business form their home, and understand the tax laws that were enacted by Congress to encourage them to do just that.

The Home-Business Tax Breaks
Passed by Congress Were
Not Accidental

They didn't unintentionally create laws that ended up decreasing Federal tax revenues. They did it for a "selfish" reason.

Look, why do banks often offer small-businesses customers exceptionally low rates on loans for business expansion? It's because, when the business does expand, the customer

- Will have lots more money to put in their bank,

- Will become a loyal long-term customer, grateful for the help the bank provided in their early-growth stages,

- Will go back to the same bank for even larger (and higher interest) loans as they continue expanding their business even further, and

- Will likely generate dozens or hundreds of new banking customers from the business's employee base.

So, was the bank altruistic in providing a low-interest, collateral-free business expansion loan? Hardly! They simply make a shrewd business decision. They helped the small customer in the short-run, so that the bank would have a large, financially strong customer in the long-run.

That is exactly why the United States Congress passed an array of tax incentives to encourage taxpayers to establish home-businesses.

This is why is the government wants to help "subsidize" your small business by giving you a large number of substantial tax breaks. They're hoping your little business will thrive and become a **BIG business** – because then you will be paying far more in taxes, but at that point, you won't mind, because you'll also be keeping far more!

It's just like investors buying stock in tiny start-up companies that have little or no net worth. Why do they do it? Because they're hoping their $1 per share investment will enable the company to grow big and profitable, increasing the worth of their investment to $20 or $200 or $2,000 per share.

Believe me the government **wants** your tax money! They're simply risking a short-term decrease in tax revenue from you, in hopes of a dramatic increase in tax revenues from you when your business is financially successful.

151

How Much Can YOU Save in Taxes?

Almost everyone will save at least 50-times the price of this book, and many people will actually cut their taxes by at least $5,000 or more!

Let's add up all the new tax-deductions you can qualify for – the money you'll be able to shift from Uncle Sam's pocket, back into our own pocket, where it belongs.

Flip back to page 69. How many dollars worth of personal expenses did you calculate you'll be able to convert into tax-deductible business expenses? The number is probably at least $10,000, and may be as high as $40,000 for some people. **Record that number on line "A" on the page 155.**

Will you hire your children as employees of your home business? If so, how many kids, and how much will you pay them? Remember, you can pay each child up to $4,700 this year, tax-deductible to you and tax-free top them.
Put this number on line "B" on page 155.

Will you be employing a spouse in your business, and giving him/her self-insured medical/dental benefits as discussed in Chapter VI? This strategy lets you tax-deduct all the out-of-pocket medical
152

related expenses you now pay in after-tax dollars. Expenses like annual deductibles, co-pays, non-covered medications, medical devises and procedures, etc. This should be worth at least a few hundred dollars, and very well could be worth thousands. **Put that number, less any payroll tax costs, on line "C" on page 155.**

Look back at Chapter VII again. How much will you be able to write-off for business use of your vehicle(s)? At a bare minimum, it will be the number of business miles times 36.5¢/mile (in 2002). For most people, this might come out somewhere between $3,500 - $5,000. **Put it on line "E."**

Will you entertain businesses associates in or outside our home? Will you qualify to write-off club dues or season tickets, etc? **Half of that number goes on line "F."**

Finally, add up all other deductions that didn't fall into one of these six categories, **and record the total on line "G."**

Let's add them up…

For special rates on filing Amended Returns (Form 1040X) to receive a refund on overpaid taxes from the past 3 years, see page 203.

YOUR Estimated Reduction in Taxes
Due to Operating a Home-Business

A. Home-related Business expenses $ _____

B. Wages for hiring children $ _____

C. Family's out-of-pock medical costs $ _____

D. Vehicle Business Miles x 36.5¢/mile $ _____

E. Business Travel (vacations) $ _____

F. 50% of Entertainment, theater, etc. $ _____

G. Other Deductions (business equipment, $ _____
loss on sale of home/car, depreciation, etc.)

Estimated Total Deductions $ _____

Are you shocked and in disbelief at that number? Most people are totally blown-away!

This is how much of your hard-earned money you've been over-paying on your taxes!

155

156

Chapter XIV

Get THOUSANDS in REFUNDS on
Tax Returns You Filed Up to *3 Years Ago*!

THIS CHAPTER COULD GET YOU AN IMMEDIATE TAX REFUND WORTH THOUSANDS OF DOLLARS!

Did you have a home-based business prior to this year, and miss-out on many of the legal tax deductions revealed in this book?

Does it make you angry to think of all the extra money that you gave Uncle Sam, just because you didn't know the things you've learned from this book?

> **Here's some good news!** You have up to three years to file an Amended Return any time you discover errors or oversights on a previous year's Tax Return!

You have until April 15, 2003 to file an Amended Return for tax-year 1999, for example, or April 15, 2004 to Amend your 2000 Return, since those dates are three years after the deadline for filing those Tax Returns. AND you can file Amended Returns for 2001 as well. You deadlines may be even later if you filed an extension or paid your tax late.

Have you already filed your current year Tax Returns, and now you're kicking yourself? File an Amended Return immediately! You can file an Amended Return even before you receive any claimed refund, and even if you've just paid "Taxes Due" on your current Returns.

If you have had a qualifying home-business in the past three years, you should immediately file Amended Returns for those years.

You could regain thousands and thousands of dollars you've over-paid in taxes, **AND the IRS will even pay you interest on the amount you overpaid!** If you overpaid by $3,000 in each of those years, for example, the IRS will send you a refund check for $9,000 **plus interest**.

Use IRS Form 1040**X** and, in Part II ("Explanation of Changes to Income, Deductions, and Credits"), simply fill-in: "Missed Business Deductions when Filing Original Form."

Filing an Amended Return can put thousands of "lost" dollars into your pocket. Yes, Christmas can come any time of the year.

May you have many happy 'Returns!'

APPENDICES

It's How Much You KEEP, That Counts! <u>Not</u> how much you <u>Make</u>
Second Edition © 2001

Appendix A

IRS Form SS-4
Application for Employer Identification Number
(EIN)

In order to employ your spouse or children in your home based business, you'll need an Employer Identification Number (EIN). You can get one quickly and at no cost by filling out and submitting a Form SS-4 with the IRS.

Although you will not be required to withhold or pay any taxes on family-member employees, you will need to file Employer's Quarterly Tax Returns. This is "just paperwork," but it is easy paperwork and, most importantly, it is the paperwork that qualifies you for all the tax breaks discussed in Chapter VI of this book.

Once you have an Employer Identification Number, the IRS will automatically send you a form each calendar-quarter to file taxes (if required), and a toll-free 800-number to call for answers to any questions about filing the form.

More information is available directly from the IRS's web site (**www.IRS.gov**), which is very user-friendly.

162

Form **SS-4**

(Rev. April 2000)

Department of the Treasury
Internal Revenue Service

Application for Employer Identification Number

(For use by employers, corporations, partnerships, trusts, estates, churches, government agencies, certain individuals, and others. See instructions.)

▶ Keep a copy for your records.

EIN

OMB No. 1545-0003

Please type or print clearly.

1 Name of applicant (legal name) (see instructions)

2 Trade name of business (if different from name on line 1)

3 Executor, trustee, "care of" name

4a Mailing address (street address) (room, apt., or suite no.)

5a Business address (if different from address on lines 4a and 4b)

4b City, state, and ZIP code

5b City, state, and ZIP code

6 County and state where principal business is located

7 Name of principal officer, general partner, grantor, owner, or trustor—SSN or ITIN may be required (see instructions) ▶ _____

8a Type of entity (Check only one box.) (see instructions)

Caution: *If applicant is a limited liability company, see the instructions for line 8a.*

☐ Sole proprietor (SSN) _____
☐ Partnership   ☐ Personal service corp.
☐ REMIC   ☐ National Guard
☐ State/local government   ☐ Farmers' cooperative
☐ Church or church-controlled organization
☐ Other nonprofit organization (specify) ▶ _____
☐ Other (specify) ▶

☐ Estate (SSN of decedent) _____
☐ Plan administrator (SSN) _____
☐ Other corporation (specify) ▶ _____
☐ Trust
☐ Federal government/military
(enter GEN if applicable) _____

8b If a corporation, name the state or foreign country (if applicable) where incorporated

State	Foreign country

9 Reason for applying (Check only one box.) (see instructions)
☐ Started new business (specify type) ▶_____
_____
☐ Hired employees (Check the box and see line 12.)
☐ Created a pension plan (specify type) ▶

☐ Banking purpose (specify purpose) ▶ _____
☐ Changed type of organization (specify new type) ▶ _____
☐ Purchased going business
☐ Created a trust (specify type) ▶ _____
☐ Other (specify) ▶

10 Date business started or acquired (month, day, year) (see instructions)

11 Closing month of accounting year (see instructions)

12 First date wages or annuities were paid or will be paid (month, day, year). **Note:** *If applicant is a withholding agent, enter date income will first be paid to nonresident alien. (month, day, year)* . . . . ▶

13 Highest number of employees expected in the next 12 months. **Note:** *If the applicant does not expect to have any employees during the period, enter -0-. (see instructions)* . . . . . ▶

Nonagricultural	Agricultural	Household

14 Principal activity (see instructions) ▶

15 Is the principal business activity manufacturing? . . . . ☐ Yes ☐ No
If "Yes," principal product and raw material used ▶

16 To whom are most of the products or services sold? Please check one box.   ☐ Business (wholesale)
☐ Public (retail)   ☐ Other (specify) ▶   ☐ N/A

17a Has the applicant ever applied for an employer identification number for this or any other business? . . . . . ☐ Yes ☐ No
Note: *If "Yes," please complete lines 17b and 17c.*

17b If you checked "Yes" on line 17a, give applicant's legal name and trade name shown on prior application, if different from line 1 or 2 above.
Legal name ▶   Trade name ▶

17c Approximate date when and city and state where the application was filed. Enter previous employer identification number if known.

Approximate date when filed (mo., day, year)	City and state where filed	Previous EIN

Under penalties of perjury, I declare that I have examined this application, and to the best of my knowledge and belief, it is true, correct, and complete.

Business telephone number (include area code)
(   )

Fax telephone number (include area code)
(   )

Name and title (Please type or print clearly.) ▶

Signature ▶   Date ▶

Note: *Do not write below this line. For official use only.*

Please leave blank ▶	Geo.	Ind.	Class	Size	Reason for applying

For Privacy Act and Paperwork Reduction Act Notice, see page 4.   Cat. No. 16055N   Form **SS-4** (Rev. 4-2000)

General Instructions

Section references are to the Internal Revenue Code unless otherwise noted.

Purpose of Form

Use Form SS-4 to apply for an employer identification number (EIN). An EIN is a nine-digit number (for example, 12-3456789) assigned to sole proprietors, corporations, partnerships, estates, trusts, and other entities for tax filing and reporting purposes. The information you provide on this form will establish your business tax account.

Caution: *An EIN is for use in connection with your business activities only. Do **not** use your EIN in place of your social security number (SSN).*

Who Must File

You must file this form if you have not been assigned an EIN before and:

● You pay wages to one or more employees including household employees.

● You are required to have an EIN to use on any return, statement, or other document, even if you are not an employer.

● You are a withholding agent required to withhold taxes on income, other than wages, paid to a nonresident alien (individual, corporation, partnership, etc.). A withholding agent may be an agent, broker, fiduciary, manager, tenant, or spouse, and is required to file **Form 1042**, Annual Withholding Tax Return for U.S. Source Income of Foreign Persons.

● You file **Schedule C,** Profit or Loss From Business, **Schedule C-EZ,** Net Profit From Business, or **Schedule F,** Profit or Loss From Farming, of **Form 1040,** U.S. Individual Income Tax Return, **and** have a Keogh plan or are required to file excise, employment, or alcohol, tobacco, or firearms returns.

The following must use EINs even if they do not have any employees:

● State and local agencies who serve as tax reporting agents for public assistance recipients, under Rev. Proc. 80-4, 1980-1 C.B. 581, should obtain a separate EIN for this reporting. See **Household employer** on page 3.

● Trusts, except the following:

1. Certain grantor-owned trusts. (See the **Instructions for Form 1041,** U.S. Income Tax Return for Estates and Trusts.)

2. Individual retirement arrangement (IRA) trusts, unless the trust has to file **Form 990-T,** Exempt Organization Business Income Tax Return. (See the **Instructions for Form 990-T.**)

● Estates

● Partnerships

● REMICs (real estate mortgage investment conduits) (See the **Instructions for Form 1066,** U.S. Real Estate Mortgage Investment Conduit (REMIC) Income Tax Return.)

● Corporations

● Nonprofit organizations (churches, clubs, etc.)

● Farmers' cooperatives

● Plan administrators (A plan administrator is the person or group of persons specified as the administrator by the instrument under which the plan is operated.)

When To Apply for a New EIN

New Business. If you become the new owner of an existing business, **do not** use the EIN of the former owner. **If you already have an EIN, use that number.** If you do not have an EIN, apply for one on this form. If you become the "owner" of a corporation by acquiring its stock, use the corporation's EIN.

Changes in Organization or Ownership. If you already have an EIN, you may need to get a new one if either the organization or ownership of your business changes. If you incorporate a sole proprietorship or form a partnership, you must get a new EIN. However, **do not** apply for a new EIN if:

● You change only the name of your business,

● You elected on **Form 8832,** Entity Classification Election, to change the way the entity is taxed, or

● A partnership terminates because at least 50% of the total interests in partnership capital and profits were sold or exchanged within a 12-month period. (See Regulations section 301.6109-1(d)(2)(iii).) The EIN for the terminated partnership should continue to be used.

Note: *If you are electing to be an "S corporation," be sure you file **Form 2553,** Election by a Small Business Corporation.*

File Only One Form SS-4. File only one Form SS-4, regardless of the number of businesses operated or trade names under which a business operates. However, each corporation in an affiliated group must file a separate application.

EIN Applied for, But Not Received. If you do not have an EIN by the time a return is due, write "Applied for" and the date you applied in the space shown for the number. **Do not** show your social security number (SSN) as an EIN on returns.

If you do not have an EIN by the time a tax deposit is due, send your payment to the Internal Revenue Service Center for your filing area. (See **Where To Apply** below.) Make your check or money order payable to "United States Treasury" and show your name (as shown on Form SS-4), address, type of tax, period covered, and date you applied for an EIN. Send an explanation with the deposit.

For more information about EINs, see **Pub. 583,** Starting a Business and Keeping Records, and **Pub. 1635,** Understanding Your EIN.

How To Apply

You can apply for an EIN either by mail or by telephone. You can get an EIN immediately by calling the Tele-TIN number for the service center for your state, or you can send the completed Form SS-4 directly to the service center to receive your EIN by mail.

Application by Tele-TIN. Under the Tele-TIN program, you can receive your EIN by telephone and use it immediately to file a return or make a payment. To receive an EIN by telephone, complete Form SS-4, then call the Tele-TIN number listed for your state under **Where To Apply.** The person making the call must be authorized to sign the form. (See **Signature** on page 4.)

An IRS representative will use the information from the Form SS-4 to establish your account and assign you an EIN. Write the number you are given on the upper right corner of the form and sign and date it.

Mail or fax (facsimile) the signed Form SS-4 within 24 hours to the Tele-TIN Unit at the service center address for your state. The IRS representative will give you the fax number. The fax numbers are also listed in Pub. 1635.

Taxpayer representatives can receive their client's EIN by telephone if they first send a fax of a completed **Form 2848,** Power of Attorney and Declaration of Representative, or **Form 8821,** Tax Information Authorization, to the Tele-TIN unit. The Form 2848 or Form 8821 will be used solely to release the EIN to the representative authorized on the form.

Application by Mail. Complete Form SS-4 at least 4 to 5 weeks before you will need an EIN. Sign and date the application and mail it to the service center address for your state. You will receive your EIN in the mail in approximately 4 weeks.

Where To Apply

The Tele-TIN numbers listed below will involve a long-distance charge to callers outside of the local calling area and can be used only to apply for an EIN. **The numbers may change without notice.** Call 1-800-829-1040 to verify a number or to ask about the status of an application by mail.

If your principal business, office or agency, or legal residence in the case of an individual, is located in: ▼	Call the Tele-TIN number shown or file with the Internal Revenue Service Center at: ▼
Florida, Georgia, South Carolina	Attn: Entity Control Atlanta, GA 39901 770-455-2360
New Jersey, New York (New York City and counties of Nassau, Rockland, Suffolk, and Westchester)	Attn: Entity Control Holtsville, NY 00501 516-447-4955
New York (all other counties), Connecticut, Maine, Massachusetts, New Hampshire, Rhode Island, Vermont	Attn: Entity Control Andover, MA 05501 978-474-9717
Illinois, Iowa, Minnesota, Missouri, Wisconsin	Attn: Entity Control Stop 6800 2306 E. Bannister Rd. Kansas City, MO 64999 816-926-5999
Delaware, District of Columbia, Maryland, Pennsylvania, Virginia	Attn: Entity Control Philadelphia, PA 19255 215-516-6999
Indiana, Kentucky, Michigan, Ohio, West Virginia	Attn: Entity Control Cincinnati, OH 45999 859-292-5467

Kansas, New Mexico, Oklahoma, Texas	Attn: Entity Control Austin, TX 73301 512-460-7843
Alaska, Arizona, California (counties of Alpine, Amador, Butte, Calaveras, Colusa, Contra Costa, Del Norte, El Dorado, Glenn, Humboldt, Lake, Lassen, Marin, Mendocino, Modoc, Napa, Nevada, Placer, Plumas, Sacramento, San Joaquin, Shasta, Sierra, Siskiyou, Solano, Sonoma, Sutter, Tehama, Trinity, Yolo, and Yuba), Colorado, Idaho, Montana, Nebraska, Nevada, North Dakota, Oregon, South Dakota, Utah, Washington, Wyoming	Attn: Entity Control Mail Stop 6271 P.O. Box 9941 Ogden, UT 84201 801-620-7645
California (all other counties), Hawaii	Attn: Entity Control Fresno, CA 93888 559-452-4010
Alabama, Arkansas, Louisiana, Mississippi, North Carolina, Tennessee	Attn: Entity Control Memphis, TN 37501 901-546-3920
If you have no legal residence, principal place of business, or principal office or agency in any state	Attn: Entity Control Philadelphia, PA 19255 215-516-6999

Specific Instructions

The instructions that follow are for those items that are not self-explanatory. Enter N/A (nonapplicable) on the lines that do not apply.

Line 1. Enter the legal name of the entity applying for the EIN exactly as it appears on the social security card, charter, or other applicable legal document.

Individuals. Enter your first name, middle initial, and last name. If you are a sole proprietor, enter your individual name, not your business name. Enter your business name on line 2. Do not use abbreviations or nicknames on line 1.

Trusts. Enter the name of the trust.

Estate of a decedent. Enter the name of the estate.

Partnerships. Enter the legal name of the partnership as it appears in the partnership agreement. **Do not** list the names of the partners on line 1. See the specific instructions for line 7.

Corporations. Enter the corporate name as it appears in the corporation charter or other legal document creating it.

Plan administrators. Enter the name of the plan administrator. A plan administrator who already has an EIN should use that number.

Line 2. Enter the trade name of the business if different from the legal name. The trade name is the "doing business as" name.

Note: *Use the full legal name on line 1 on all tax returns filed for the entity. However, if you enter a trade name on line 2 and choose to use the trade name instead of the legal name, enter the trade name on all returns you file. To prevent processing delays and errors, **always** use either the legal name only or the trade name only on all tax returns.*

Line 3. Trusts enter the name of the trustee. Estates enter the name of the executor, administrator, or other fiduciary. If the entity applying has a designated person to receive tax information, enter that person's name as the "care of" person. Print or type the first name, middle initial, and last name.

Line 7. Enter the first name, middle initial, last name, and SSN of a principal officer if the business is a corporation; of a general partner if a partnership; of the owner of a single member entity that is disregarded as an entity separate from its owner; or of a grantor, owner, or trustor if a trust. If the person in question is an alien individual with a previously assigned individual taxpayer identification number (ITIN), enter the ITIN in the space provided, instead of an SSN. You are not required to enter an SSN or ITIN if the reason you are applying for an EIN is to make an entity classification election (see Regulations section 301.7701-1 through 301.7701-3), and you are a nonresident alien with no effectively connected income from sources within the United States.

Line 8a. Check the box that best describes the type of entity applying for the EIN. If you are an alien individual with an ITIN previously assigned to you, enter the ITIN in place of a requested SSN.

Caution: *This is not an election for a tax classification of an entity. See "Limited liability company (LLC)" below.*

If not specifically mentioned, check the "Other" box, enter the type of entity and the type of return that will be filed (for example, common trust fund, Form 1065). Do not enter N/A. If you are an alien individual applying for an EIN, see the **Line 7** instructions above.

Sole proprietor. Check this box if you file Schedule C, C-EZ, or F (Form 1040) and have a qualified plan, or are required to file excise, employment, or alcohol, tobacco, or firearms returns, or are a payer of gambling winnings. Enter your SSN (or ITIN) in the space provided. If you are a nonresident alien with are a nonresident alien with no effectively

connected income from sources within the United States, you do not need to enter an SSN or ITIN.

REMIC. Check this box if the entity has elected to be treated as a real estate mortgage investment conduit (REMIC). See the Instructions for Form 1066 for more information.

Other nonprofit organization. Check this box if the nonprofit organization is other than a church or church-controlled organization and specify the type of nonprofit organization (for example, an educational organization).

If the organization also seeks tax-exempt status, you must file either **Package 1023,** Application for Recognition of Exemption, or **Package 1024,** Application for Recognition of Exemption Under Section 501(a). Get **Pub. 557,** Tax Exempt Status for Your Organization, for more information.

Group exemption number (GEN). If the organization is covered by a group exemption letter, enter the four-digit GEN. (Do not confuse the GEN with the nine-digit EIN.) If you do not know the GEN, contact the parent organization. Get Pub. 557 for more information about group exemption numbers.

Withholding agent. If you are a withholding agent required to file Form 1042, check the "Other" box and enter "Withholding agent."

Personal service corporation. Check this box if the entity is a personal service corporation. An entity is a personal service corporation for a tax year only if:

● The principal activity of the entity during the testing period (prior tax year) for the tax year is the performance of personal services substantially by employee-owners, and

● The employee-owners own at least 10% of the fair market value of the outstanding stock in the entity on the last day of the testing period.

Personal services include performance of services in such fields as health, law, accounting, or consulting. For more information about personal service corporations, see the **Instructions for Forms 1120 and 1120-A,** and **Pub. 542,** Corporations.

Limited liability company (LLC). See the definition of limited liability company in the **Instructions for Form 1065,** U.S. Partnership Return of Income. An LLC with two or more members can be a partnership or an association taxable as a corporation. An LLC with a single owner can be an association taxable as a corporation or an entity disregarded as an entity separate from its owner. See Form 8832 for more details.

Note: *A domestic LLC with at least two members that does not file Form 8832 is classified as a partnership for Federal income tax purposes.*

● If the entity is classified as a partnership for Federal income tax purposes, check the "partnership" box.

● If the entity is classified as a corporation for Federal income tax purposes, check the "Other corporation" box and write "limited liability co." in the space provided.

● If the entity is disregarded as an entity separate from its owner, check the "Other" box and write in "disregarded entity" in the space provided.

Plan administrator. If the plan administrator is an individual, enter the plan administrator's SSN in the space provided.

Other corporation. This box is for any corporation other than a personal service corporation. If you check this box, enter the type of corporation (such as insurance company) in the space provided.

Household employer. If you are an individual, check the "Other" box and enter "Household employer" and your SSN. If you are a state or local agency serving as a tax reporting agent for public assistance recipients who become household employers, check the "Other" box and enter "Household employer agent." If you are a trust that qualifies as a household employer, you do not need a separate EIN for reporting tax information relating to household employees; use the EIN of the trust.

QSub. For a qualified subchapter S subsidiary (QSub) check the "Other" box and specify "QSub."

Line 9. Check only **one** box. Do not enter N/A.

Started new business. Check this box if you are starting a new business that requires an EIN. If you check this box, enter the type of business being started. **Do not** apply if you already have an EIN and are only adding another place of business.

Hired employees. Check this box if the existing business is requesting an EIN because it has hired or is hiring employees and is therefore required to file employment tax returns. **Do not** apply if you already have an EIN and are only hiring employees. For information on the applicable employment taxes for family members, see **Circular E,** Employer's Tax Guide (Publication 15).

Created a pension plan. Check this box if you have created a pension plan and need an EIN for reporting purposes. Also, enter the type of plan.

Note: *Check this box if you are applying for a trust EIN when a new pension plan is established.*

Banking purpose. Check this box if you are requesting an EIN for banking purposes only, and enter the banking purpose (for example, a bowling league for depositing dues or an investment club for dividend and interest reporting).

Changed type of organization. Check this box if the business is changing its type of organization, for example, if the business was a sole proprietorship and has been incorporated or has become a partnership. If you check this box, specify in the space provided the type of change made, for example, "from sole proprietorship to partnership."

Purchased going business. Check this box if you purchased an existing business. **Do not** use the former owner's EIN. **Do not** apply for a new EIN if you already have one. Use your own EIN.

Created a trust. Check this box if you created a trust, and enter the type of trust created. For example, indicate if the trust is a nonexempt charitable trust or a split-interest trust.

Note: Do not check this box if you are applying for a trust EIN when a new pension plan is established. Check "Created a pension plan."

Exception. Do **not** file this form for certain grantor-type trusts. The trustee does not need an EIN for the trust if the trustee furnishes the name and TIN of the grantor/owner and the address of the trust to all payors. See the Instructions for Form 1041 for more information.

Other (specify). Check this box if you are requesting an EIN for any other reason, and enter the reason.

Line 10. If you are starting a new business, enter the starting date of the business. If the business you acquired is already operating, enter the date you acquired the business. Trusts should enter the date the trust was legally created. Estates should enter the date of death of the decedent whose name appears on line 1 or the date when the estate was legally funded.

Line 11. Enter the last month of your accounting year or tax year. An accounting or tax year is usually 12 consecutive months, either a calendar year or a fiscal year (including a period of 52 or 53 weeks). A calendar year is 12 consecutive months ending on December 31. A fiscal year is either 12 consecutive months ending on the last day of any month other than December or a 52-53 week year. For more information on accounting periods, see **Pub. 538**, Accounting Periods and Methods.

Individuals. Your tax year generally will be a calendar year.

Partnerships. Partnerships generally must adopt one of the following tax years:
● The tax year of the majority of its partners,
● The tax year common to all of its principal partners,
● The tax year that results in the least aggregate deferral of income, or
● In certain cases, some other tax year.

See the Instructions for Form 1065 for more information.

REMIC. REMICs must have a calendar year as their tax year.

Personal service corporations. A personal service corporation generally must adopt a calendar year unless:
● It can establish a business purpose for having a different tax year, or
● It elects under section 444 to have a tax year other than a calendar year.

Trusts. Generally, a trust must adopt a calendar year except for the following:
● Tax-exempt trusts,
● Charitable trusts, and
● Grantor-owned trusts.

Line 12. If the business has or will have employees, enter the date on which the business began or will begin to pay wages. If the business does not plan to have employees, enter N/A.

Withholding agent. Enter the date you began or will begin to pay income to a nonresident alien. This also applies to individuals who are required to file Form 1042 to report alimony paid to a nonresident alien.

Line 13. For a definition of agricultural labor (farmwork), see **Circular A,** Agricultural Employer's Tax Guide (Publication 51).

Line 14. Generally, enter the exact type of business being operated (for example, advertising agency, farm, food or beverage establishment, labor union, real estate agency, steam laundry, rental of coin-operated vending machine, or investment club). Also state if the business will involve the sale or distribution of alcoholic beverages.

Governmental. Enter the type of organization (state, county, school district, municipality, etc.).

Nonprofit organization (other than governmental). Enter whether organized for religious, educational, or humane purposes, and the principal activity (for example, religious organization—hospital, charitable).

Mining and quarrying. Specify the process and the principal product (for example, mining bituminous coal, contract drilling for oil, or quarrying dimension stone).

Contract construction. Specify whether general contracting or special trade contracting. Also, show the type of work normally performed (for example, general contractor for residential buildings or electrical subcontractor).

Food or beverage establishments. Specify the type of establishment and state whether you employ workers who receive tips (for example, lounge—yes).

Trade. Specify the type of sales and the principal line of goods sold (for example, wholesale dairy products, manufacturer's representative for mining machinery, or retail hardware).

Manufacturing. Specify the type of establishment operated (for example, sawmill or vegetable cannery).

Signature. The application must be signed by (a) the individual, if the applicant is an individual, (b) the president, vice president, or other principal officer, if the applicant is a corporation, (c) a responsible and duly authorized member or officer having knowledge of its affairs, if the applicant is a partnership or other unincorporated organization, or (d) the fiduciary, if the applicant is a trust or an estate.

How To Get Forms and Publications

Phone. You can order forms, instructions, and publications by phone 24 hours a day, 7 days a week. Just call 1-800-TAX-FORM (1-800-829-3676). You should receive your order or notification of its status within 10 workdays.

Personal computer. With your personal computer and modem, you can get the forms and information you need using IRS's Internet Web Site at **www.irs.gov** or File Transfer Protocol at **ftp.irs.gov.**

CD-ROM. For small businesses, return preparers, or others who may frequently need tax forms or publications, a CD-ROM containing over 2,000 tax products (including many prior year forms) can be purchased from the National Technical Information Service (NTIS).

To order **Pub. 1796,** Federal Tax Products on CD-ROM, call **1-877-CDFORMS** (1-877-233-6767) toll free or connect to **www.irs.gov/cdorders**

Recordkeeping	. 7 min.
Learning about the law or the form	. 22 min.
Preparing the form	. 46 min.
Copying, assembling, and sending the form to the IRS . . .	. 20 min.

Second Edition © 2001

Appendix B

Employment Contract
for Hiring Family Members

Make copies of the following fill-in-the-blanks form or develop your own, and complete a separate one for each family member you will employ in your home-business.

You have many options for establishing wages.

- If you establish an hourly rate, you will determine pay and document work performed by using simple timesheets.

- If you an established weekly wage for a set quantity of work to be performed (such as mow lawn or clean house), you will specify, in writing, the work to be performed, and the employee will document each time the tasks are completed.

- Especially for hiring your spouse, you could designate the wage as being "__% of the profits of the business, paid annually upon filing of business tax returns."

In all cases, however, you'll need to:

- Establish that the wage you pay is reasonable and customary in your geographic location.

- Obtain documentation that the work was performed (timesheets, employee invoices, work-log, etc.)

- Document that the wages were paid (always pay by check, preferably on a separate business account).

This applies to Chapter VI.

168

Employment Agreement

As of _____, _____ agrees to
(effective date)   (name of employer)

employ _____ to perform duties
                        (name of employee)

as specified below, subject to change from time to time as mutually agreed in writing, and subject to curtailment at any time at the employer's sole discretion.

1. Duties shall include:

_____
_____
_____
_____
_____
_____
_____
_____
_____
_____
_____
_____
_____
_____

2. Term. This agreement shall begin on the effective date specified above and shall continue until terminated by either party upon written two-weeks-advance notice to the other.

169

3. Compensation. Pay shall be <u>weekly/biweekly/monthly</u>

(select by striking-through <u>two (2)</u> of the above)

according to the option checked below:

☐ $_____ per hour, upon submission completed timesheets, with a maximum of _____ hours per pay-period specified above.

☐ $_____ per pay period, upon submission of log showing that all duties specified in this contract were performed.

☐   _____ percent of net profit of the business, paid annually within 30 days of filing of Business Income Tax Returns.

4. Additional Compensation. If work is offered, agreed to, and performed outside of the scope specified in Para. 1, or as amended, additional remuneration shall be as mutually agreed by both parties.

5. Expenses. The employee is expected to promote the employer's business as a part of his or her on-going duties, and thus may incur expenses from time to time for entertainment, meals, travel, club dues, etc. All such expenditures, if pre-approved by employer, will be reimbursed within 30 days of submission of Claim for Reimbursement of Employee-Incurred Business Expenses, along with required receipts/documentation.

6. Vacation. The employee shall be entitled to take _____ days vacation per year, during which time compensation <u>will/will-not</u>

(strike through one)

be paid.

7. Disability. If employee is unable to perform his/her duties for a period of two consecutive weeks due to illness or incapacity, his/her

170

compensation will continue at a rate 25% less than full-compensation, for a period of up to six months. Vacation will continue to accrue during this absence. Upon return to full employment, full compensation will be reinstated.

8. Employment-at-Will. This is an employment-at-will agreement, meaning that the employer has the right to terminate this agreement at any time for any reason, or for no reason, upon giving the employee at least two (2) weeks written notice.

9. Severance Clause. If termination is for any reason other than for-cause, two weeks compensation shall be provided on the final day of employment, as a severance fee.

10. Entire Agreement. This document, plus any attached and co-signed Addenda, shall serve as the entire agreement between the two parties.

AGREED AND ACCEPTED:

_____   _____
(EMPLOYER)   (EMPLOYEE)

_____   _____
(DATE)   (DATE)

172

Appendix C

Self-Insured Medical Reimbursement Plan

Use the following form (edit it as necessary to fit your circumstances) to provide certain medical benefits to your family-member employees, and their family (that's how you get covered).

This applies to Chapter VI.

Self-Insured Medical Reimbursement Plan

Effective _____, _____

(DATE)　　　　　　　　　(YOUR COMPANY NAME)

hereby establishes the following Health and Accident Reimbursement Plan for the exclusive benefit of its employees. This Plan is to be considered "Secondary Coverage" for those employees who are covered under any other Medical Insurance Plan or Plans.

1. Reimbursement for Medical Expenses.

(a.) As of date of employment, per Employment Contract, all employees of _____, whether employed

(YOUR COMPANY NAME)

full-time or part-time, qualify to be reimbursed for all Medical Care expenses incurred by the employee and not eligible for coverage under any other Insurance Plan(s) in effect at the time the cost(s) was/were incurred. This Plan is to be considered Secondary Coverage, for reimbursement purposes.

(b.) For purposes of this Plan, Medical Expenses shall be defined by IRS Code, Section 213(d).

(c.) This Plan also covers any employee's spouse and the employee's legal dependents, as defined in IRS Code, Section 152.

(d.) For minor employees, defined as employees less than 18 years of age, any and all benefits due under this Plan will be made payable to the parent or legal guardian of the employee.

(e.) In lieu of providing reimbursement for expenses for which the employee or his/her dependent would be eligible under this Plan, the employer may, at his/her option, elect to pay the expenses directly to the service provider.

175

(f.) Benefits under this Plan shall be limited to $_____ per eligible person per Plan Year.

2. Continuation of Compensation During Periods of Disability.

(a.) **Short Term Disability**. Effective immediately upon employment, should an employee covered under this Plan become disabled and unable to perform his/her duties as specified in his/her Employment Agreement, his/her Compensation will continue at a rate of twenty-five (25) percent less than full Compensation, for a period of up to six (6) months.

(b.) **Long Term Disability.** If disability continues for more than six (6) months, employer shall, beginning in the seventh month, pay the employee at a rate of fifty (50) percent of his/her normal, full Compensation, until the Employee is able to return to work, or for one year, whichever comes first.

3. Secondary Coverage.

(a.) As previously stated and alluded to, eligibility for reimbursement under this Plan shall be limited to such amounts as not covered under any other Medical Insurance Plan under which the employee/ dependent is covered and/or any government Medical Reimbursement Plan under which the employee/ dependent is covered.

176

4. Covered Medical Expenses.

(a.) In addition to costs customarily considered to be "medical expenses," this Plan also included costs for annual eye exams, reading glasses, contact lenses and/or surgery to correct vision; routine dental check-ups, and any and all necessary and required dental preventive care, repair and restoration; and outpatient or inpatient treatment for chemical dependency, drug/alcohol abuse and psychiatric disorders.

5. Termination and Amendments to this Plan.

(a.)   The employer may, at his sole discretion, elect to terminate or modify this Plan for any reason.

(b.)   Any termination of this Plan or changes or modifications thereto, shall be communicated to all covered employees in writing at least sixty (60) days prior to the effective date of the termination or change in coverage.

6. IRS Exclusions.

(a.)   It is the intent of the provider of this Medical Coverage that all medical benefits paid to an eligible employee under this Plan shall be eligible for exclusion from the gross income of the employee and/or his/her parent or legal guardian, as provided for in Sections 105 and 106 of the Internal Revenue Code.

Employee Acknowledgement:

I have read this employee benefit entitled Self-Insured Medical Reimbursement Plan and I understand how it applies to me personally.

_____
(Employee's Signature)

_____
(Date of Signing

_____
(Employee's Printed Name)

Appendix D

Vehicle-Use Log

Make lots of copies of the following Vehicle-Use Log, and always keep spare ones handy in any vehicle(s) you will be using for your business.

If you keep your Vehicle-Use Log in a place where you always see it when entering the vehicle (on the dash, on the console, etc.) and always have a pen or pencil with it, you won't forget to fill it out and you can reduce this to about a 3-second chore.

Remember, this little bit of paperwork is earning you a $1,000 deduction for every 3,000 business miles you drive, every time your car moves. That's thousands in deductions by the end of each year.

This related to Chapter VIII.

Vehicle Use Log

Date	Destination	Purpose	Starting Odometer Reading	Ending Odometer Reading	Total Miles Traveled	Expenses Incurred (gas, tolls, etc.)

182

Appendix E

IRS Form W-4 (2002)
Employee Withholding Allowance Form

Complete the following Form, using these instructions:

Ignore the top two-thirds of the following form (it is for taxpayers who take Standard Deductions, rather than Itemizing, which you, as a home-business owner, will be doing).

Print your personal data on lines 1, 2 and 3.

Go back to page 145 and find the number you arrived at in the very bottom line of the Worksheet, and **insert that number on line 5 on the Form W-4.**

Leave lines 6 and 7 blank.

Sign and date where indicated.

Leave lines 8, 9 and 10 blank (your employer will complete these lines).

Take this Revised Form W-4 to your employer's payroll office, and hand it in, saying simply that your tax situation has changed so you would like this revised form to replace the one you have on file.

Form W-4 (2002)

Purpose. Complete Form W-4 so your employer can withhold the correct Federal income tax from your pay. Because your tax situation may change, you may want to refigure your withholding each year.

Exemption from withholding. If you are exempt, complete only lines 1, 2, 3, 4, and 7 and sign the form to validate it. Your exemption for 2002 expires February 16, 2003. See **Pub. 505**, Tax Withholding and Estimated Tax.

Note: *You cannot claim exemption from withholding if (a) your income exceeds $750 and includes more than $250 of unearned income (e.g., interest and dividends) and (b) another person can claim you as a dependent on their tax return.*

Basic instructions. If you are not exempt, complete the **Personal Allowances Worksheet** below. The worksheets on page 2 adjust your withholding allowances based on itemized deductions, certain credits, adjustments to

income, or two-earner/two-job situations. Complete all worksheets that apply. **However, you may claim fewer (or zero) allowances.**

Head of household. Generally, you may claim head of household filing status on your tax return only if you are unmarried and pay more than 50% of the costs of keeping up a home for yourself and your dependent(s) or other qualifying individuals. See line E below.

Tax credits. You can take projected tax credits into account in figuring your allowable number of withholding allowances. Credits for child or dependent care expenses and the child tax credit may be claimed using the **Personal Allowances Worksheet** below. See **Pub. 919**, How Do I Adjust My Tax Withholding? for information on converting your other credits into withholding allowances.

Nonwage income. If you have a large amount of nonwage income, such as interest or dividends, consider making estimated tax payments using **Form 1040-ES**, Estimated Tax for Individuals. Otherwise, you may owe additional tax.

Two earners/two jobs. If you have a working spouse or more than one job, figure the total number of allowances you are entitled to claim on all jobs using worksheets from only one Form W-4. Your withholding usually will be most accurate when all allowances are claimed on the Form W-4 for the highest paying job and zero allowances are claimed on the others.

Nonresident alien. If you are a nonresident alien, see the **Instructions for Form 8233** before completing this Form W-4.

Check your withholding. After your Form W-4 takes effect, use **Pub. 919** to see how the dollar amount you are having withheld compares to your projected total tax for 2002. See **Pub. 919**, especially if you used the **Two-Earner/Two-Job Worksheet** on page 2 and your earnings exceed $125,000 (Single) or $175,000 (Married).

Recent name change? If your name on line 1 differs from that shown on your social security card, call 1-800-772-1213 for a new social security card.

Personal Allowances Worksheet (Keep for your records.)

A Enter "1" for **yourself** if no one else can claim you as a dependent . . . . **A** _____

B Enter "1" if: {
- You are single and have only one job; or
- You are married, have only one job, and your spouse does not work; or
- Your wages from a second job or your spouse's wages (or the total of both) are $1,000 or less. } . . **B** _____

C Enter "1" for your **spouse.** But, you may choose to enter "-0-" if you are married and have either a working spouse or more than one job. (Entering "-0-" may help you avoid having too little tax withheld.) . . . . **C** _____

D Enter number of **dependents** (other than your spouse or yourself) you will claim on your tax return . . . . . . **D** _____

E Enter "1" if you will file as **head of household** on your tax return (see conditions under **Head of household** above) . **E** _____

F Enter "1" if you have at least $1,500 of **child or dependent care expenses** for which you plan to claim a credit . . **F** _____
   (**Note:** Do **not** include child support payments. See **Pub. 503**, Child and Dependent Care Expenses, for details.)

G **Child Tax Credit** (including additional child tax credit):
- If your total income will be between $15,000 and $42,000 ($20,000 and $65,000 if married), enter "1" for each eligible child plus **1 additional** if you have three to five eligible children or **2 additional** if you have six or more eligible children.
- If your total income will be between $42,000 and $80,000 ($65,000 and $115,000 if married), enter "1" if you have one or two eligible children, "2" if you have three eligible children, "3" if you have four eligible children, or "4" if you have five or more eligible children.   **G** _____

H Add lines A through G and enter total here. **Note:** *This may be different from the number of exemptions you claim on your tax return.* ▶ **H** _____

For accuracy, complete all worksheets that apply. {
- If you plan to **itemize or claim adjustments to income** and want to reduce your withholding, see the **Deductions and Adjustments Worksheet** on page 2.
- If you have **more than one job** or are **married and you and your spouse both work** and the combined earnings from all jobs exceed $35,000, see the **Two-Earner/Two-Job Worksheet** on page 2 to avoid having too little tax withheld.
- If **neither** of the above situations applies, **stop here** and enter the number from line H on line 5 of Form W-4 below.
}

- **Cut here and give Form W-4 to your employer. Keep the top part for your records.** -

Form W-4
Department of the Treasury
Internal Revenue Service

Employee's Withholding Allowance Certificate

▶ **For Privacy Act and Paperwork Reduction Act Notice, see page 2.**

OMB No. 1545-0010

2002

1 Type or print your first name and middle initial Last name	2 Your social security number

Home address (number and street or rural route)	3 ☐ Single ☐ Married ☐ Married, but withhold at higher Single rate.
	Note: *If married, but legally separated, or spouse is a nonresident alien, check the "Single" box.*

City or town, state, and ZIP code	4 If your last name differs from that on your social security card, check here. You must call 1-800-772-1213 for a new card. ▶ ☐

5 Total number of allowances you are claiming (from line **H** above **or** from the applicable worksheet on page 2) . . . . **5** _____

6 Additional amount, if any, you want withheld from each paycheck . . . . **6** $ _____

7 I claim exemption from withholding for 2002, and I certify that I meet **both** of the following conditions for exemption:
- Last year I had a right to a refund of **all** Federal income tax withheld because I had **no** tax liability **and**
- This year I expect a refund of **all** Federal income tax withheld because I expect to have **no** tax liability.
   If you meet both conditions, write "Exempt" here . . . . ▶ **7** _____

Under penalties of perjury, I certify that I am entitled to the number of withholding allowances claimed on this certificate, or I am entitled to claim exempt status.

Employee's signature
(Form is not valid unless you sign it.) ▶ _____   **Date** ▶ _____

8 Employer's name and address (Employer: Complete lines 8 and 10 only if sending to the IRS.)	9 Office code (optional)	10 Employer identification number

Cat. No. 10220Q

Deductions and Adjustments Worksheet

Note: *Use this worksheet only if you plan to itemize deductions, claim certain credits, or claim adjustments to income on your 2002 tax return.*

1 Enter an estimate of your 2002 itemized deductions. These include qualifying home mortgage interest, charitable contributions, state and local taxes, medical expenses in excess of 7.5% of your income, and miscellaneous deductions. (For 2002, you may have to reduce your itemized deductions if your income is over $137,300 ($68,650 if married filing separately). See **Worksheet 3** in Pub. 919 for details.) . . . **1** $ _____

2 Enter:
{
$7,850 if married filing jointly or qualifying widow(er)
$6,900 if head of household
$4,700 if single
$3,925 if married filing separately
} . . . . **2** $ _____

3 **Subtract** line 2 from line 1. If line 2 is greater than line 1, enter "-0-" . . . . **3** $ _____

4 Enter an estimate of your 2002 adjustments to income, including alimony, deductible IRA contributions, and student loan interest **4** $ _____

5 **Add** lines 3 and 4 and enter the total. Include any amount for credits from **Worksheet 7** in Pub. 919. . **5** $ _____

6 Enter an estimate of your 2002 nonwage income (such as dividends or interest) . . . . **6** $ _____

7 **Subtract** line 6 from line 5. Enter the result, but not less than "-0-" . . . . **7** $ _____

8 **Divide** the amount on line 7 by $3,000 and enter the result here. Drop any fraction . . . . . . **8** _____

9 Enter the number from the **Personal Allowances Worksheet, line H,** page 1 . . . . **9** _____

10 **Add** lines 8 and 9 and enter the total here. If you plan to use the **Two-Earner/Two-Job Worksheet,** also enter this total on line 1 below. Otherwise, **stop here** and enter this total on Form W-4, line 5, page 1 . **10** _____

Two-Earner/Two-Job Worksheet

Note: *Use this worksheet only if the instructions under line H on page 1 direct you here.*

1 Enter the number from line H, page 1 (or from line 10 above if you used the **Deductions and Adjustments Worksheet**) **1** _____

2 Find the number in **Table 1** below that applies to the **lowest** paying job and enter it here **2** _____

3 If line 1 is **more than or equal to** line 2, subtract line 2 from line 1. Enter the result here (if zero, enter "-0-") and on Form W-4, line 5, page 1. **Do not** use the rest of this worksheet . . . . **3** _____

Note: *If line 1 is **less than** line 2, enter "-0-" on Form W-4, line 5, page 1. Complete lines 4–9 below to calculate the additional withholding amount necessary to avoid a year end tax bill.*

4 Enter the number from line 2 of this worksheet . . . . **4** _____

5 Enter the number from line 1 of this worksheet . . . . **5** _____

6 **Subtract** line 5 from line 4 . . . . **6** _____

7 Find the amount in **Table 2** below that applies to the **highest** paying job and enter it here . . . . . **7** $ _____

8 **Multiply** line 7 by line 6 and enter the result here. This is the additional annual withholding needed . . **8** $ _____

9 Divide line 8 by the number of pay periods remaining in 2002. For example, divide by 26 if you are paid every two weeks and you complete this form in December 2001. Enter the result here and on Form W-4, line 6, page 1. This is the additional amount to be withheld from each paycheck . . . . **9** $ _____

Table 1: Two-Earner/Two-Job Worksheet

Married Filing Jointly				All Others			
If wages from **LOWEST** paying job are—	Enter on line 2 above	If wages from **LOWEST** paying job are—	Enter on line 2 above	If wages from **LOWEST** paying job are—	Enter on line 2 above	If wages from **LOWEST** paying job are—	Enter on line 2 above
$0 - $4,000	0	44,001 - 50,000	8	$0 - $6,000	0	75,001 - 95,000	8
4,001 - 9,000	1	50,001 - 55,000	9	6,001 - 11,000	1	95,001 - 110,000	9
9,001 - 15,000	2	55,001 - 65,000	10	11,001 - 17,000	2	110,001 and over	10
15,001 - 20,000	3	65,001 - 80,000	11	17,001 - 23,000	3		
20,001 - 25,000	4	80,001 - 95,000	12	23,001 - 28,000	4		
25,001 - 32,000	5	95,001 - 110,000	13	28,001 - 38,000	5		
32,001 - 38,000	6	110,001 - 125,000	14	38,001 - 55,000	6		
38,001 - 44,000	7	125,001 and over	15	55,001 - 75,000	7		

Table 2: Two-Earner/Two-Job Worksheet

Married Filing Jointly		All Others	
If wages from **HIGHEST** paying job are—	Enter on line 7 above	If wages from **HIGHEST** paying job are—	Enter on line 7 above
$0 - $50,000	$450	$0 - $30,000	$450
50,001 - 100,000	800	30,001 - 70,000	800
100,001 - 150,000	900	70,001 - 140,000	900
150,001 - 270,000	1,050	140,001 - 300,000	1,050
270,001 and over	1,150	300,001 and over	1,150

Appendix F

Your Business Plan DRAFT

Most Business Plans are long and complex. But the short one that follows meets all criteria required by the IRS for proving:

1. **That you have a legitimate BUSINESS**, not a hobby, thus protecting you from the "hobby-loss rule."

2. **That your business is based in your HOME**, thus protecting you from the "exclusive use" restrictions of "home office" rules.

3. **That you have an INTENT to produce a profit**, which allows you to write-off net business losses, year after year if necessary.

What follows is just a draft. Feel free to modify it, expand it, edit it, and make it more specific so that it accurately reflects your current and future business activity.

Note: Let's say your business is selling a nutrition product line. You might be tempted to call your business something like "Feel Better, Live Longer."

Later, you might develop an additional, totally separate line of business, in which you help people write better resumes, and you call it "Killer Resumes that Get You in the Door."

Since these are separate business, you would be expected to file two separate Schedule C's with each Tax Return.

Or you could (which I highly recommend) establish a broader business name, such as, in my case, Mueller Enterprises. A broader name like that allows the flexibility to add, delete and change the mix of business lines, and to file only one Schedule C.

Essentially, each "business" is treated, for tax purposes, as if it were a separate department within one company. If you decide to stop doing one of your activities, you will have closed down a department of your company, but not your Company.

That makes thing much simpler, and has lots of tax advantages.

Business Plan

of

(Name of Your Company)

established on

(Month, Date & Year)

by

(Your Name)

Principal

(insert Your Mailing Address)
(Your Telephone number, Fax number, E-mail address)

Business Plan

Table of Contents

Business Plan

of

(Name of Your Company) ®

a Sole-Proprietorship Business registered by (Your Name) in the State of (your State) .

Vision Statement

(Your Company Name)®, founded in **(insert year)** as a home-based business, intends to profitably mass market a growing number of products and services to the general buying public. Due to low product prices, high retail profit margins, large target audiences, and the tax advantages available to me by running this as a home-based businesses, I intend to produce a substantial profit, over a period of time.

Mission Statement

(Insert Name of Business) will provide top-quality products and services at the best prices to my customers through personal sales, direct-marketing, paid and/or non-paid advertising, in-home product demonstrations, catalog sales, online promotion, fundraising support, etc.

In order to achieve my Vision, I have educated myself fully on the products and services I will provide, and on the target audiences to whom I will sell.

Target Prospects

The ideal target prospects for my company's products/services fall into these broad categories:

- Xxxxxxxxxxxxxxxxxxxxxxxxxxxxxxxxxxxxxxxxxxxxxxxxxxxx
xxxxxxxxxxxxxxxxxxxxxxxxxxxxxxxxxxxxxxxxxxxxxxxxxxxxxxxx
xxxxxxxxxxxxxxxxxxxxxxxxxxxxxxxxxxxxxxxxxxxxxxxxxxxxxxxx
xxxxxxxxxxxxxxxxxxxxxxxxxx..

- Yyyyyyyyyyyyyyyyyyyyyyyyyyyyyyyyyyyyyyyyyyyyyyyyyyyy
yyyyyyyyyyyyyyyyyyyyyyyyyyyyyyyyyyyyyyyyyyyyyyyyyyyyyyyy
yyyyyyyyyyyyyyyyyyyyyyyyyyyyyyyyyyyyyyyyyyyyyyyyyyyyyyyy
yyyyyyyyyyyyyyyyyyyyyyyyyyyyyyyy.

- Zzzzzzzzzzzzzzzzzzzzzzzzzzzzzzzzzzzzzzzzzzzzzzzzzzzzzzzz
zzzzzzzzzzzzzzzzzzzzzzzzzzzzzzzzzzzzzzzzzzzzzzzzzzzzzzzzzz
zzzzzzzzzzzzzzzzzzzzzzzzzzzzzzzzz.

Customer Profiles

The ideal Customer possesses these qualities and/or needs:
- 11111111111111111111111111111111
- 2222222222222222222222222222222222
- 33333333333333333333333333333, and
- 4444444444444444444444444.

Competitive Environment

Competitors include XXXXXXXXXXX, Inc., which provides xxxxxxxxx, YYYYYYYYYYYYY, Inc. whose product line includes xxxxxxxxxxxxxxxxx, and ZZZZZZZZZZZZ, Inc. whose advantage is xxxxxxxxxxxx.

Our Marketing Advantage

In order to successfully sell against our competitors, we will offer
xxxxxxxxxxxxxxxxxxxxxxxxxxx
xxxxxxxxxxxxxxxxxxxxxxxxxxxxxxxxxxxxxxxxxxxxxxxxxxxxxxxxxxxxxx
xxxxxxxxxxxxxxxxxxxxxxxxxxxxxxxxxxxxxxxxxxxxxxxxxxxxxxxxxxxxxx
xxxxxxxxxxxxxxxxxxxxxxxxxxxxxxxxxxxxxxxxxxxxxxxxxxxxxxxxxxxxxx
xxxxxxxxxxxxxxxxxxxxxxxxxxxxxxxxxxxxxxxxxxxxxxxxxxxxxxxxxxxxxx
xxxxxxxxxxxxxxxxxxxxxxxxxxxxxxxxxxxxxxxxxxxxxxxxxx.

Marketing Plan

(Your Company's Name)'s marketing strategy is to aggressively promote
_____ products and services, on a
local/statewide/regional/nationwide **(state one or more)** basis through retail
customers, friends, relatives, business associates, and new prospects generated
through direct mail, advertising and all other direct marketing approaches,
capitalizing on the fact that we offer three distinct benefits:

    A. Aaaaaaaaaaaaaaaaaaaaaaaaa
    B. Bbbbbbbbbbbbbbbbb, and
    C. Cccccccccccccccccccccccccccccccc.

Therefore, the daily modus operandi of the President & Chief Executive Officer
of **(Insert Name of Your Company)** will be to promote the business starting
with a prospecting or sales call as his/her first stop upon leaving his/her business
location (i.e., home) each day, continuing as possible throughout the day, and
ending each evening with a final prospecting or sales call. This will include:

- Prospecting and making price comparisons at various merchant establishments rather than simply "shopping,"

- Prospecting and promoting my company's products and services whenever playing golf, fishing or other social or sporting activities conducive to business discussions;

- Promoting my company's products/services at church, school and numerous other appropriate functions.

193

Sales Strategies

Because of the universal appeal of my company's product lines, low prices, and unique sales advantages we will capitalize on with the following retail sales strategies:

Direct Sales:
Many of my retail customers with entrepreneurial potential will be converted to product distributors by simply showing them the tax advantages of owning their own business and how they can also save by buying products at wholesale for personal use and retail sale.

Gift Giving:
Once recipients of gift certificates contact me for redemption, I will offer them the opportunity to convert to Independent Marketing Associate or Distributor status in order to enjoy even lower product costs. Duplication of this process will lead to hundreds and then to thousands of new customers who might then convert to independent distributor status and duplicate the process over and over.

Fundraising:
I will provide FREE membership in my organization to any bona fide not-for-profit organization in order to help them establish, promote and conduct a successful fundraising program. As a Member, the organization may order products at wholesale price and sell at retail; and if they choose to become an Independent Distributor, they may sponsor other Independent Distributors or organizations and enjoy commissions and bonus qualifications on the total volume of their sales organization.

One of the unique and effective programs for fundraising groups is to simply order gift certificates at 50% off retail, then sell them within their group at 25% off. Once the recipients contact them for redemption, they may also offer the recipients the opportunity to convert to Independent Distributor status in order to enjoy the much lower product costs. Duplication of this process will lead to hundreds and then thousands of new customers who would then convert to Independent Distributor status and duplicate the process over and over.

Networkers:

Experts say that between 10-million and 15-million Americans are involved in network marketing today. Most are with companies that sell good quality, but generally overpriced products. My company's low prices and substantial advantages mean that these millions of experienced networkers are prime candidates for my business opportunity.

Direct-Mail Advertising:

In order to reach the millions of experienced networkers outlined above, as well as tens of millions other people interested in reducing their taxes legally, morally and ethically, I will aggressively conduct a Direct Mail marketing program as a part of my marketing efforts.

Classified Advertising:

In order to reach the millions of potential retail buyers as well as potential Independent Distributors, we will explore the use of various forms of Classified Advertising to seek out prospects.

Word-of-Mouth:

Since the most effective and most highly credible form of advertising is word-of-mouth advertising from satisfied customers, we will compensate our current customers to provide us references to new prospective customers.

Media Exposure:

Since it is possible to make the success of our company and the products we sell to appear "newsworthy" and to be of "human interests," we will attempt to interest local broadcast and print media in providing "free advertising" for our company and our products.

In-Home Sales Meetings:

Recognizing that the products and services provided by **(insert name of your Company)** will be of benefit and of interest to the President's own friends, family, contacts, former customers/clients, acquaintances, neighbors, colleagues, fellow civic club members, former employers and employees, vendors, suppliers, etc., in-home presentation meetings are planned.

Conclusion

(**Name of company**) will establish a track record of cost-effective products, excellent support and exemplary service to our customers. Their expressions of satisfaction and encouragement will become numerous.

The products and services offered and marketed by **(Name of company)** will continue to expand and diversify over time, to eventually encompass a wide array of profitable business entities, operating under the umbrella name of **(Name of company).**

Following an initial period of start-up losses, **(Name of company)** intends to become a highly profitable, tax-paying business entity.

Appendix G

The tax deductions you have just read about, also apply to the past three years. If you had a home-based business in any of those years and failed to claim deductions that you now know you qualified for, you can file an Amended Return for any or all of those years, reclaiming up to thousands of dollars in overpaid taxes, plus interest.

Of course you may not be able to claim <u>all</u> of those 'lost' deductions because you may not have kept the necessary documentation. But consult a tax preparer who is experienced in home-business tax-law, because sometimes you can claim some of the 'lost' deductions even though you may only partial documentation.

The form you would file is a 1040X like the following example.

Form **1040X**
(Rev. November 2001)

Department of the Treasury—Internal Revenue Service

Amended U.S. Individual Income Tax Return

▶ See separate instructions.

OMB No. 1545-0091

This return is for calendar year ▶ _____ , or fiscal year ended ▶ _____

Please print or type

Your first name and initial	Last name	Your social security number
If a joint return, spouse's first name and initial	Last name	Spouse's social security number
Home address (no. and street) or P.O. box if mail is not delivered to your home	Apt. no.	Phone number ( )
City, town or post office, state, and ZIP code. If you have a foreign address, see page 2 of the instructions.		For Paperwork Reduction Act Notice, see page 6.

A If the name or address shown above is different from that shown on the original return, check here . . . . ▶ ☐

B Has the original return been changed or audited by the IRS or have you been notified that it will be? . . ☐ **Yes** ☐ **No**

C Filing status. Be sure to complete this line. **Note.** You cannot change from joint to separate returns after the due date.

On original return ▶ ☐ Single ☐ Married filing joint return ☐ Married filing separate return ☐ Head of household ☐ Qualifying widow(er)

On this return ▶ ☐ Single ☐ Married filing joint return ☐ Married filing separate return ☐ Head of household* ☐ Qualifying widow(er)

* If the qualifying person is a child but not your dependent, see page 2.

Use Part II on the Back to Explain any Changes

		A. Original amount or as previously adjusted (see page 2)	**B.** Net change— amount of increase or (decrease)— explain in Part II	**C.** Correct amount
Income and Deductions (see pages 2–6)				
1 Adjusted gross income (see page 3)	**1**			
2 Itemized deductions or standard deduction (see page 3) . .	**2**			
3 Subtract line 2 from line 1	**3**			
4 Exemptions. If changing, fill in Parts I and II on the back	**4**			
5 Taxable income. Subtract line 4 from line 3	**5**			
Tax Liability				
6 Tax (see page 4). Method used in col. C _____	**6**			
7 Credits (see page 4)	**7**			
8 Subtract line 7 from line 6. Enter the result but not less than zero .	**8**			
9 Other taxes (see page 4)	**9**			
10 Total tax. Add lines 8 and 9	**10**			
Payments				
11 Federal income tax withheld and excess social security and RRTA tax withheld. If changing, see page 4	**11**			
12 Estimated tax payments, including amount applied from prior year's return	**12**			
13 Earned income credit (EIC)	**13**			
14 Additional child tax credit from Form 8812	**14**			
15 Credits from Form 2439 or Form 4136	**15**			
16 Amount paid with request for extension of time to file (see page 4)				**16**
17 Amount of tax paid with original return plus additional tax paid after it was filed				**17**
18 Total payments. Add lines 11 through 17 in column C				**18**
Refund or Amount You Owe				
19 Overpayment, if any, as shown on original return or as previously adjusted by the IRS . . .				**19**
20 Subtract line 19 from line 18 (see page 5)				**20**
21 **Amount you owe.** If line 10, column C, is more than line 20, enter the difference and see page 5 .				**21**
22 If line 10, column C, is less than line 20, enter the difference				**22**
23 Amount of line 22 you want **refunded to you**				**23**
24 Amount of line 22 you want **applied to your** estimated tax	**24**			

Sign Here

Joint return?
See page 2.
Keep a copy for your records.

Under penalties of perjury, I declare that I have filed an original return and that I have examined this amended return, including accompanying schedules and statements, and to the best of my knowledge and belief, this amended return is true, correct, and complete. Declaration of preparer (other than taxpayer) is based on all information of which the preparer has any knowledge.

▶ _____ Your signature   Date _____

▶ _____ Spouse's signature. If a joint return, **both** must sign.   Date _____

Paid Preparer's Use Only

Preparer's signature ▶	Date	Check if self-employed ☐	Preparer's SSN or PTIN
Firm's name (or yours if self-employed), address, and ZIP code ▶		EIN	
		Phone no. ( )	

Cat. No. 11360L

Form **1040X** (Rev. 11-2001)

Part I   **Exemptions.** See Form 1040 or 1040A instructions.

If you are **not changing your exemptions,** do not complete this part.
If claiming **more exemptions,** complete lines 25–31.
If claiming **fewer exemptions,** complete lines 25–30.

			A. Original number of exemptions reported or as previously adjusted	B. Net change	C. Correct number of exemptions
25	Yourself and spouse	25			
	Caution. If your parents (or someone else) can claim you as a dependent (even if they chose not to), you cannot claim an exemption for yourself.				
26	Your dependent children who lived with you	26			
27	Your dependent children who did not live with you due to divorce or separation	27			
28	Other dependents	28			
29	Total number of exemptions. Add lines 25 through 28	29			
30	Multiply the number of exemptions claimed on line 29 by the amount listed below for the tax year you are amending. Enter the result here and on line 4.	30			

Tax year	Exemption amount	But see the instructions for line 4 on page 3 if the amount on line 1 is over:
2001	$2,900	$99,725
2000	2,800	96,700
1999	2,750	94,975
1998	2,700	93,400

31   Dependents (children and other) not claimed on original (or adjusted) return:

(a) First name Last name	(b) Dependent's social security number	(c) Dependent's relationship to you	(d) ✓ if qualifying child for child tax credit (see page 5)
			☐
			☐
			☐
			☐
			☐
			☐

No. of your children on line 31 who:

- lived with you . . ▶ ☐

- **did not** live with you due to divorce or separation (see page 5). . ▶ ☐

Dependents on line 31 not entered above ▶ ☐

Part II   **Explanation of Changes to Income, Deductions, and Credits**

Enter the line number from the front of the form for each item you are changing and give the reason for each change. Attach only the supporting forms and schedules for the items changed. If you do not attach the required information, your Form 1040X may be returned. Be sure to include your name and social security number on any attachments.

If the change relates to a net operating loss carryback or a general business credit carryback, attach the schedule or form that shows the year in which the loss or credit occurred. See page 2 of the instructions. Also, check here . . . . . ▶ ☐

Part III   **Presidential Election Campaign Fund.** Checking below will not increase your tax or reduce your refund.

If you did not previously want $3 to go to the fund but now want to, check here . . . . ▶ ☐
If a joint return and your spouse did not previously want $3 to go to the fund but now wants to, check here . . . . ▶ ☐

Dear Friend,

Thank you for reading and using this tax-reduction system. Everyone should pay his or her fair share of taxes, but <u>no one</u> should pay <u>more</u> than his or her fair share, and that's why I wrote this book.

This book is <u>now</u> available in book stores. To order additional copies at a special reorder price please see the final page of this book, contact us at <u>Info@HomeBusinessTaxSavings.com</u>, or call us at 1-410-956-9562. If you, or someone you know, would be interested in making this book available to groups of people who need this information, you could earn a generous commission, while helping people you know.

For details about becoming a re-seller of this book, please contact us directly at <u>Info@HomeBusinessTaxSavings.com</u>.

Ronald R. Mueller
Author

FREE HELP and INFORMATION

☐   **<u>YOU QUALIFY</u> to *<u>automatically</u>* receive FREE tax-change updates and tax savings tips. To subscribe to our free newsletter, *Tax Tips You Can Bank On*, just go to our web site at <u>www.HomeBusinessTaxSavings.com</u> and enter your email address in the pop-up window.**

☐   If you had a home-based business in *<u>any of the past three years</u>*, <u>you probably qualify for a Big Refund</u> from the IRS. Owners of this book can get Special Rates for review of your past Tax Returns and for preparing Amended Returns (Form 1040X) to claim refunds for deductions you never know you qualified for. Send an email to <u>Info@HomeBusinessTaxSavings.com</u> and ask for specifics.

☐   **If you're looking for a <u>tax-preparer</u> who *<u>specializes</u>* in Home-Business Tax-Law, we'll be happy to make a recommendation. Just send an email to <u>Info@HomeBusinessTaxSavings.com</u>.**

☐   If you'd like us to <u>recommend some home-based businesses</u> that allow you to maximize your tax deductions, send an email to <u>Info@HomeBusinessTaxSavings.com</u>

☐   **If you're looking for someone to <u>help you with a tax audit</u>, or would like to hear about "<u>audit protection insurance</u>," send us an email at <u>www.HomeBusinessTaxSavings.com</u>.**

☐   If you know <u>groups of people who need this book</u>, we will give you a generous 40% referral fee for telling them about it. Learn all about our two-tiered Affiliate program by visiting our web site at <u>www.HomeBusinessTaxSavings.com</u>.

Use the order form on the reverse side to obtain additional copies of *It's How Much You KEEP, That Counts! Not how much you Make* -- THE ULTIMATE TAX-REDUCTION SYSTEM for Small and Home Based Businesses.

Quick Order Form
FOR ADDITIONAL COPIES OF THIS BOOK

INTERNET Orders: http://www.HomeBusinessTaxSavings.com

FAX Orders: 1-410-956-2068

TELEPHONE Orders: 1-410-956-9562

E-MAIL Orders: Info@HomeBusinessTaxSavings.com

MAIL Orders: **Triple-7 Publishing**
Post Office Box 1117
Edgewater, MD 21037-7117

Reorder Price:

- eBook version: **$37.00** for immediate download
- **Printed & Bound edition:**   **$49.00**
  ($37+$12 for Printing, Binding, Production & Shipping)

NAME: _____

MAILING ADDRESS: _____

CITY: _____ STATE: _____ ZIP: _____

PHONE: _____ FAX: _____

E-MAIL (For FREE LIFETIME updates): _____

I am ordering the: E-Book ($37.00): ____   Print Version ($49.00 total): _____

Payment Information (for MAIL orders and FAX orders):

☐ **My Check or Money Order is Enclosed for $_____**

☐ **Please charge my Credit Card for $_____**

Please check one: ☐ **MasterCard**   ☐ **Visa**   ☐ **AmEx**   ☐ **Discover**

Card Number: _____ Exp. Date: ___/___

It's How Much You KEEP, That Counts! Not how much you Make.
Second Edition © 2001

Use the order form on the reverse side to obtain additional copies of *It's How Much You KEEP, That Counts! Not how much you Make* -- THE ULTIMATE TAX-REDUCTION SYSTEM for Small and Home Based Businesses.

Quick Order Form
FOR ADDITIONAL COPIES OF THIS BOOK

INTERNET Orders: http://www.HomeBusinessTaxSavings.com

FAX Orders: 1-410-956-2068

TELEPHONE Orders: 1-410-956-9562

E-MAIL Orders: Info@HomeBusinessTaxSavings.com

MAIL Orders: Triple-7 Publishing
Post Office Box 1117
Edgewater, MD 21037-7117

Reorder Price:

- **eBook version:**   **$37.00** for immediate download
- **Printed & Bound edition:**   **$49.00**
  ($37+$12 for Printing, Binding, Production & Shipping)

NAME: _____

MAILING ADDRESS: _____

CITY: _____ STATE: _____ ZIP: _____

PHONE: _____ FAX: _____

E-MAIL (For FREE LIFETIME updates): _____

I am ordering the: E-Book ($37.00): _____   Print Version ($49.00 total): _____

Payment Information (for MAIL orders and FAX orders):

☐ **My Check or Money Order is Enclosed for $_____**

☐ **Please charge my Credit Card for $_____**

Please check one: ☐ **MasterCard**   ☐ **Visa**   ☐ **AmEx**   ☐ **Discover**

Card Number: _____ Exp. Date: ___/___

It's How Much You KEEP, That Counts! Not how much you Make.
Second Edition   © 2001